BRIDGE YOUR GAP

Sales Strategies and Systems
for Becoming a Top Financial Advisor

By Jim Effner

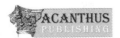

© 2018 Jim Effner. All rights reserved.

No part of this book may be reproduced or transmitted in any form or by any means, electronic or mechanical, including photocopying, recording, or by any information storage and retrieval system, without written permission of the author, except for the inclusion of brief quotations in a review.

Published by Acanthus Publishing, Brookline, Massachusetts.

ISBN: 978-0-9754810-1-1

Interior Design by Kodi Bobo

DISCLAIMER

This publication is designed to provide accurate and authoritative information with regard to the subject matter covered. It is sold with the understanding that the publisher is not engaged in rendering legal, accounting, or other professional advice. If legal advice or other expert assistance is required, the services of a competent professional should be sought.

The author does not endorse or advise on the sale of financial products to individual consumers (e.g., life insurance, annuities, stocks, bonds, mutual funds, or other similar products). Please note that neither the information presented nor any opinion expressed is to be considered as an offer to buy or purchase any insurance or securities products and services referenced in this book.

Table of Contents

Table of Contents V

Acknowledgments VII

Sales Cycle Mastery Illustration XI

Introduction XIII

Chapter 1: HOW I GOT into the BUSINESS 1

Chapter 2: MY HEARING LOSS 21

Chapter 3: A NEW BEGINNING 41

Chapter 4: DEVELOPING MY SYSTEM 53

Chapter 5: THE GAP – WHAT IS "THE GAP?" 59

Photos From My Life and Career 71

Chapter 6: PROSPECTING 83

Chapter 7: PHONING and CALENDAR MANAGEMENT 103

Chapter 8: FACT-FINDING 125

Chapter 9: PLANNING 155

Chapter 10: IMPLEMENTATION 191

Chapter 11: ANNUAL REVIEW 223

FINAL NOTE: NOW YOU'RE READY 249

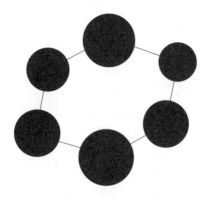

Acknowledgments

As I sit back and think about this book, all the people who played such a significant role in my career and in the creation of this book come to mind.

From the start, my General Agent Bill Beckley, wow, what an impact you had!! To all the veteran reps in my original office – Tom, Gregg, Pat, Dave, Lou, Jack, John, Jim, and Lee – who gave me so much and taught me invaluable lessons, thank you!

To my mentor, Todd, and my classmates I started with (Rajer, Andrew, Ross, Tim, and Tim), you guys are the best and helped me so much. To all my NML rep friends – Wags, CW, Ira, Joe, and so many more – thanks for helping me think big and expect so much more. To my M.P. study group, the Research Council, you guys were the best and so impactful. Thank you so much.

In my new journey, with the P2P Group, I couldn't have done it without three people. I want to thank Jennifer for her belief in me and her uncanny ability to turn my ideas into tangible curriculums; Kelly, for her never-ending positive attitude and passion for the work she does; Luke, for his creative ability to take my vision and turn it into a first-class brand with everything he does.

From the beginning, I was so lucky to be born into my family. I want to thank my Mom and Dad, along with all four of my siblings: Sue, Randy, Bob, and Mary. In all of your own unique ways, you provided family values wrapped around a strong Christian faith. I can't thank you enough and I love you all.

Throughout this entire journey, there was one rock, one guiding star, that always kept me grounded, was far more mature and responsible, and, without her, I had no chance. That's my beautiful wife, Lynn. Although I received many accolades throughout my career, everyone who is anyone knows you are the one who deserves them all! I love you so much.

To my kids, Brittney, Briana, and Bryce. You are my inspiration. Thank you for being who you are. I am so proud of each of you. You always have given me such a reason to be the best I can possibly be. The love I have for each of you is beyond what I thought was possible. What a gift you have been!

Thank you, reader, for investing your time, energy, and resources into this book and having the desire for personal and professional growth. It's up to you to take the next step and apply these principles in your career and life. I am confident that they can help you transform your true potential into real performance.

Last, but not least, I want to thank my Lord and Savior, Jesus Christ. Without Him, and the faith He has given me, none of this, or anything, would be possible.

BRIDGE YOUR GAP • JIM EFFNER

x

TRANSFORM YOUR
TRUE POTENTIAL
INTO REAL PERFORMANCE

BRIDGE YOUR GAP • JIM EFFNER

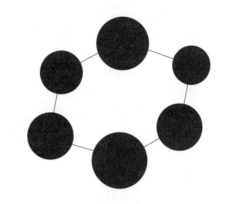

Introduction

Welcome to *Bridge Your Gap: Sales Strategies and Systems for Becoming a Top Financial Advisor*. I'm so glad you chose to read this book. Writing this book has been one of my lifelong bucket list items, and I couldn't be happier to have completed it. Let me first explain what to expect as you continue reading.

I have divided this book into two components, and the first component has two sections. The first section will be largely inspirational and will dovetail two different aspects of my professional and personal experiences; these detail my 30 years of experiences in the financial planning industry. My aim here is to inspire you to understand the opportunity at your fingertips when you become the master of your craft. I also share a couple of times in my life when I experienced great adversity. In these experiences, the outcome was the exact opposite of what I expected. I share these stories to help individuals facing adversity to understand that there is a silver lining to every dark cloud. Your success is always up to you and sometimes what you think could be one of the most disastrous situations can evolve into one of the greatest experiences of your life. You'll see this theme illustrated in my story and I hope you can relate it to yours.

The second component of this book is all about execution. I believe so many people in this industry are never able to tap into their true potential. When you master the craft of financial planning and become an expert salesperson, the sky is the limit. It is my hope that you will experience 10 years' worth of growth in a very short time frame. All you have to do is follow along with me, and I will provide you with all the tools and confidence needed. However, first you must understand, then close, what I call the Gap, because the key to your unlimited success will come down to understanding and closing the Gap.

It is my hope that the first part of this book will inspire you, while the second part of the book will teach you exactly what you need to do – step by step. I know this book will be a phenomenal tool and you will gain significant knowledge and insight on your first read-through. But I also designed it to be a great reference book to keep on your shelf from the time you begin to master your craft until your last day on the job. Please, keep referencing and rereading the book throughout your career for both inspiration and practical advice. I hope you enjoy reading this book as much I enjoyed writing it. Best of luck to you!

BRIDGE YOUR GAP • JIM EFFNER

BRIDGE YOUR GAP • JIM EFFNER

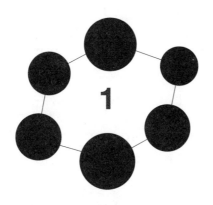

HOW I GOT
into the
BUSINESS

I grew up in a middle-class household of five children. I was number five. My four older brothers and sisters were separated by less than two years, while I was seven years younger than child number four. I joke about my birth being a mistake. My mother always says "a blessing," but I think you know the truth as you read this. I never had a chip on my shoulder because of my family dynamic. I've never needed therapy because of that, but by the time I reached adulthood, I had developed some personal traits that would later drive me to succeed.

My parents were tired by the time I came along. Been there, done that, raised four children, enforced all the rules (although they never missed one of my games and were phenomenal parents).

By age 11, all my siblings had left home and I was essentially raised as an only child. Because much of my parents' energy had gone to my elder siblings, they had little remaining in their tanks for me. By the time I came along, they simply wanted me to stay out of trouble.

But I wanted much more than just to stay out of trouble. I wanted the respect of my father and the respect of my siblings. I wanted to be noticed, and I *aspired to be somebody*. My goal was to enjoy a successful career.

I realized that I would first gain their respect by becoming only the second of the five to go directly from high school to college and graduate in four years with a bachelor's degree. Nevertheless, once I passed that milestone, my only means of earning the kind of respect I wanted would be through my career accomplishments and through the accumulation of wealth. By the time I entered college, I knew I wanted to be in some sort of high-income business. I wanted the finer things in life that only money can buy.

I don't know exactly where my desire to maintain a high standard of living originates, but I do have a few ideas.

It certainly wasn't my upbringing. My parents had a bit of a *Leave It to Beaver* mentality. They were strong Christians and family values were a huge part of their lives. Neither was motivated by money. Instead, the activities of their children, such as sporting events and family time, punctuated their roles as parents. I got away with a few things as a child, but one thing I could never do was miss the family dinner!

Being parents, being involved in the church, and playing bridge with friends – those were my parents' priorities. They had no interest in frivolous vacations, fancy cars, nice homes, or tapping into their full "income earning potential."

I can't imagine a better childhood, better parents, or better siblings, so by all means, I'm not stating this as a negative. It's just when you think about my upbringing, it is odd that I became intensely motivated to create the most significant financial living I could possibly construct.

Yet, I have a fairly good idea where the roots of that motivation took hold.

My mom loves to tell a story about me as an 11-year-old, when we pulled up to a stoplight. Alone in the backseat, I spotted a fancy car next to ours and asked my dad if we could get a car like that one the next time. He laughed at my question, saying we didn't have that kind of money.

I looked at him and asked, "Well, why don't we have that kind of money?" My dad didn't have an answer. I share this story because when I attended college as a finance major, I always tried to connect the dots as to what I could do to have an affluent lifestyle.

One of my first jobs was as a caddy at an exclusive country club, carrying bags for people who had conversations around the golf course that I didn't hear at home. I remember at age 16 working a couple of club events, valet-parking cars worth more than my mom and dad's house. To me, the lifestyle of the country club members seemed like fun, and I didn't understand why my family failed to enjoy the same things. But I certainly knew that I wanted to pursue a similar lifestyle to the country club members when I got older.

I had some obstacles in the way, the first being my C average as a student. I knew that being sought after for top jobs at investment firms meant being on a fast track to a prestigious grad school for an MBA, which required a minimum 3.5 GPA. I didn't even have a 3.0 GPA.

The second obstacle: because I grew up in a middle-class family in a middle-class neighborhood, I had no connections. I literally knew no one who made anywhere near the kind of money I dreamt of and focused on earning.

So, as I started interviewing during my senior year at Valparaiso University, I was limited to interviews suitable to my unenviable GPA. These interviews served as mere stepping stones to what I wanted. In fact, it took five other stepping stones before I ultimately could "arrive," probably in my late 30s, at the lifestyle I desperately wanted to begin as soon as possible. Frustration starts to set in when you know what you want but can't connect the dots to get there, and at that time I couldn't.

Quite honestly, the trading industry fascinated me more than any other. Being 6'6", a former athlete, loud, and good with numbers, I pictured myself standing in the pit, trading stocks and bonds. To me, the work of a stockbroker represented an energetic, fast-paced career, something I had always been attracted to, and one I knew I could make a very good living at with an aggressive approach. And if I couldn't exactly do that, I was determined to do something that offered the same kind of rarified economic rewards.

One day, while scanning the interview sign-up sheets at my college's business office, I noted that I couldn't sign up for fully two-thirds of them because of my mediocre GPA. As for the remaining third, when I went into those interviews, I literally wanted to vomit. I had never pictured myself in any of those careers throughout the four years of studying for my finance degree. Jobs like uniform salesman, fire equipment salesman, or stocking shelves in grocery stores certainly would not create a path to my desired lifestyle.

I remember signing up for an industrial sales job that sounded sexy but I soon learned that the uniform I'd be required to wear was the furthest thing from sexy. Then I noticed an interview for an insurance company (today they are referred to as financial services firms, but in 1989, the term "insurance company" obviously and appropriately applied).

I knew I needed to get as much interviewing exposure as possible. I had some flexibility in my calendar, so I signed up for the insurance interview for practice, knowing full well I had no intention of selling insurance for a living. But upon entering the interview, I began to feel the blood rush through my veins like I'd never felt about any type of career. There were many reasons I reacted this way.

The first reason was the unlimited income potential, which some companies promise without any basis. But this company showed me examples of top-producing employees earning seven figures. That was exciting!

The second reason was the fact that I didn't have to hop from one job to another, to another, to finally end up with a real job – one where I could earn a substantial income. I would actually have the real job immediately upon graduating at age 22, and if I performed well, then I could stay there for the rest of my career.

Something else that resonated with me: I immediately connected with my interviewer. I felt as if he connected with me also and that he cared about me. He asked me many personal questions, while engaging in a genuinely open dialogue, unlike the other stuffy, formal interviews I had encountered until that point.

I impressed them and got invited back for a second interview at their downtown Chicago office – the most attractive office I've ever seen in my life. I met people who lived the lifestyle that I had been dreaming about. The person who interviewed me had a private country club membership, so I shared stories about wanting somebody to carry my golf bags like all those times I had carried everybody else's. We talked about golf, we talked about cars, we talked about family, we talked about values, and we talked about a career of nobility and doing something that mattered, but at the same time a career that promised a sky-is-the-limit potential.

I started in the life insurance business on June 26, 1989. I turned 22 on June 20, 1989, so I was young and green, had zero internships, and had zero business experience. My summer jobs while at college consisted of house painting and custodial work – the extent of my experience going into the insurance business.

I don't remember if I heard this in a speech or if somebody told me, but within the first few months, it became clear to me that those who excel in the insurance field are not necessarily the smartest, most affluent or well-connected, or those with internships or sales experience who already had a leg up on me. What I learned very quickly is that the people who reach the top are those who *work the hardest.*

It was a breath of fresh air for me because I knew I might not be the smartest, the best salesman yet, or the most well connected, but there was no way I would let anyone outwork me!

During the initial few weeks, it became obvious to me that the first three to five years of this business are primarily a numbers game, centered on activity. The more referrals you get, the more phone calls you make, the more people you see, and the more insurance you sell, the greater likelihood of your success. Thus, I put myself on an activity-based, focused program and knew I had to stay on that path.

I cannot think of a luckier break than finding myself in an incredible working environment where I worked in my first office. I worked with the best of the best. There were people around me who were not only members of the

"Million Dollar Round Table (MDRT)" but also members of the more prestigious "Court of the Table" and "Top of the Table." We even had the president of the MDRT national organization, which recognizes the top 6% of producers in the life insurance industry in my local office. These individuals set the bar and set the example. I was always raised to respect my elders, but I think part of me has always looked to older men as role models.

Many people have had a significant impact on me, people I have become close to, yet some were 20 to 30 years or more my senior. The environment that I started in was full of these role models. It's one thing to be *told* that something is possible, but an entirely different matter when you see people *doing* it on a daily basis in the very office where you work.

I wanted to be one of them, but I had no patience. I certainly didn't want to wait until middle age, so it was a transformative experience to understand that I wouldn't be measured in this business on a chronological time clock, nor by seniority. I realized that my success would come through effective activity, self-discipline, focus, and willingness to get comfortable with the uncomfortable. Additionally, I knew that I had to work harder than everyone else. I knew this formula could elevate me to the top of my field, which was incredibly exciting.

The younger representatives who I mentor have often asked how I became motivated so quickly. What I can tell you is that most colleagues in my culture were 15 to 25

years my senior – the salt of the earth, people who lead by example, people I trusted, who cared about others, and people you would love to have in your community. Because of all this, I trusted them completely when they told me about the importance of life insurance, and disability insurance, and saving money. And when they shared stories of what they accomplished with their clients, I soon felt as if I had embarked on a lifelong mission.

I like to use evocative words like "mission" because these weren't services I "sold," rather I felt convinced in what I was offering, as did my colleagues, that it really felt as if I were on a mission.

My parents raised me to have integrity. Honesty is a huge core value of mine, so when you combine a tremendous work ethic and discipline with a deep sense of conviction, throw in a little seasoning I call "strong desire to be respected," and blend in a burning desire for affluence – you create a potent combination. I can't take sole credit for most of these ingredients, as these were developed along the way as part of my environment.

I started in a culture of high expectations: if you did not qualify for the Million Dollar Round Table by the end of your third year where I worked, you were terminated. I wasn't going to wait until my third year.

I bought a poster board to cover my bedroom door. From the board's lower left corner to the upper right corner, on a diagonal line, I wrote the letters "MDRT"; from the left upper corner to the lower right corner I drew another diagonal line, and I wrote "Rookie of the Year, 1990." I focused on both of those things. I looked at them every single day. There were many days I felt defeated and many days I worked long hours, but I never went to bed without walking past that chart. By the end of 1990, I qualified for the Million Dollar Round Table, and I won the prestigious rookie of the year award. (I qualified for the Million Dollar Round Table each year since entering the business, and even achieved "Court of the Table" on three separate occasions. All of this was achieved in my 20s.)

I remember the black-tie night when I attended the awards event in downtown Chicago in a rented tux. I was even invited to deliver a speech in front of what I considered the most prestigious financial organization in the world. I wasn't nervous; I was so proud of what I had achieved, but more importantly, I felt that I now *belonged*.

Unbeknownst to me, the CEO of our insurance company was a guest of honor at the awards banquet. I remember stating in my speech how fortunate I felt at the ripe old age of 22 to find a career to pursue for the rest of my life. The CEO, who spoke before me, was so moved by my speech that it compelled him to return to the stage to express how my words moved him and how much he appreciated them.

I can't stress enough how I owe my early success to so many people. I simply followed the instructions offered by my superiors. When I had questions, I went to my mentor who always helped me. When dealing with cases that I couldn't quite get my head around, I worked jointly with colleagues, who were always there for me.

I remember at the end of my first quarter hearing the

importance of learning via joint work. Henceforth, I made a point to participate in a minimum of one joint-work appointment each week. I participated in as many as four in some weeks.

During my first calendar year, I completed 84 joint-work appointments. After the 30th meeting, I felt I could sell better than some of the people that I collaborated with, which often frustrated me, but I always managed to learn one or two things from every meeting, which ultimately benefitted me down the road.

In my teaching today, you'll often hear me say that I'm not smart enough to invent original sales concepts. Every single thing I know about sales was absorbed from others through my dedication to learning and my ability to soak up information like a human sponge in the first decade of my career.

Qualifying for the Million Dollar Round Table and winning rookie of the year represented the goals that I needed to achieve in my local office. On a national level, my company also had awards for the top second- and third-year reps, and I wanted to focus on those awards next. They called those awards the bronze, the silver, and the gold, which is akin to Olympic medals. In my region, I earned runner-up in the bronze and won the silver at a national level. I finished third in the gold, so a fast start was part of my genetic makeup in this business.

So much of the material that I teach today in my program originated during my first decade in the business. Most of my material comes not from my victories, but from multiple defeats, the challenges and rejection I faced daily. When I look back at those first 10 years, I wouldn't want to go back and do it again. At the same time, I have such fond memories, and the experience molded and shaped my entire future.

It's fairly simple to dissect how I accomplished these achievements, as I've discussed the dedication to specific activities that led me to this success. Remember, my environment influenced me tremendously, in that I was lucky to be involved with great people. But I was also coachable; I never tried to reinvent the wheel, I embraced what I learned, and I simply did as I was told. It proved easier and more effective than trying to generate my own system, at least until I knew I was ready.

I think the key to rep success early in the business isn't necessarily what they accomplish in good times – almost everybody performs well when things are going well. What differentiated my early success were my accomplishments during bad times, and, boy, there were many! But even without the mistakes, there was also ample rejection, and that will eat away at most people.

Some of my mistakes included trying to chase the lifestyle and spending too much money, too quickly, and early on. I neglected to save enough for taxes, or when I had to weather the storm of a couple of bad commission runs. The financial stress that I put on myself became a burden. However, I believe that my combination of youth and utter lack of experience in the business created pressures that ultimately helped me, because my production boiled down to an obligation, rather than a choice. I would never coach anybody to do it the way I did it, but it seemed to work for me.

My teaching *Performance to Potential* (P2P) stands for taking one's current potential and transforming it into real performance. It always perplexed me as to why reps struggle in this business, knowing that most potential clients don't plan or save and are usually underinsured.

There are a plethora of opportunities out there and, to borrow a cliché, the world is your oyster. When you work with a company that has your back and you know you'll never have to apologize for the products, you can have an entire community seeking you out. I honestly don't understand how every rep out there doesn't enjoy a vibrant practice. One of the most popular questions I'm asked today is: "Jim, you were so successful early on as a financial rep, why did you get out of that for the leadership role that you ended up taking as a managing partner?"

For one, I grew bored after 12 years as a financial rep and didn't want to do it for 45 years – not because I didn't think it was worthwhile (quite the opposite – I was more convinced than ever about that), but I simply needed more intellectual stimulation.

Second, although I have positively affected the lives of several hundred investors, I wanted to have a greater impact. The fact is, once you hit a certain point, practice scalability is no longer an option. In a leadership role, by training thousands of financial reps who impact thousands of clients, I could have an exponential effect.

Another reason: one of the most influential men in my life at this time was my managing partner, Bill Beckley, and, quite frankly, I wanted to be like him. He served as a managing partner; therefore, I wanted to be a managing partner. All in all, I knew that the best of the best in the industry could earn unlimited income and have a wonderful lifestyle, whether rep or managing partner.

I also wanted my father to be proud of me. My dad was old school; he came from a corporate world where "management" meant promotion, and there he had a hierarchical link in his mind. For his son to be one of the youngest managing partners in the financial industry was a big deal to him and I knew that would make him proud. In short, there was a piece of me that wanted to achieve success for him as well.

Finally, I've always been drawn to leadership and possessed such a strong desire to lead. Had I not entered financial services, I would have become a high school basketball coach and tried to work my way up to the elite college level. Being a leader is something that comes naturally to me, and I just wasn't getting that level of fulfillment from being a rep.

Reflecting on my 14 years as a managing partner, I realized that I only spent a small percentage of my time actually teaching reps to become professional salespeople. I realized this was my strongest skill set and one of my largest passions. I knew that, when the time came to step down, passing on my knowledge and teaching would need to be a bigger part of my professional world.

I concluded that what I love doing the most, and possessed the most natural gifts for, was working with reps who had at least completed their first three years in the business and were likely to remain in this career. With my experience and skills, I had the ability to transform them into unbelievably successful reps and guide them into capitalizing on their God-given potential.

And I wanted to do it my way, with the people I wanted to do it with, and I wanted to build my own company. So, in February 2015, that was the road I chose.

So often things happen for a reason, and always for a purpose. I've always been a man of strong faith and, now, although hindsight is 20-20, I know that there was a purpose to my choice to start a company that would teach reps things that I knew they needed to be taught.

I began a journey that put together everything I had ever taught, everything I had ever learned, and everything I'd ever done throughout the entire sales cycle of a financial representative. I transferred everything in my head to chicken scratch on almost 1,000 sheets of paper, then found through a local Google search a woman who owned a small boutique marketing firm. I brought my pile of handwritten notes when we met, and she began to transcribe them into virtual documents that started to resemble the orderly fashion of a curriculum.

I realized how dependent I'd become, relying on an awesome assistant and not having to do any admin work for the past 17 years. Getting those chicken-scratch pieces of paper into Word documents to actually produce a curriculum signified a big step in the right direction.

I knew that the sales cycle would be broken down into six stages: prospecting (the fuel of our business), phoning and calendar management for the second stage, fact-finding, planning, and implementing, followed by the annual review. Once I put the manual together, I trademarked it and titled it the *Sales Cycle Mastery* program. I had yet to have a client. I spent so much time organizing the material and now had the content and clear vision, but I still had to build a business.

I realized that the best way to start would be to call a few of my most respected and longtime friends. I asked if they wanted to hire me to work with a group of four-year reps to implement my curriculum, based on my track record as a highly successful rep and respected managing partner. They gave me an opportunity, so I took on two client groups for the year 2016, which allowed me to test all the material and, through daily interaction with the groups, I constantly tested, tweaked, and added to the curriculum to get to the point that it is today.

As word spread, I received calls from others inquiring if I'd be willing to work with their reps. I've always had big visions and an abundance of confidence, yet I didn't expect this thing to catch on so quickly. I knew that in the first stage of my business I wanted to work with people face to face. I knew I only wanted to work with 10 client groups. Ultimately, I wanted to teach in the first two weeks of every month. I wanted to reserve the last two weeks of the month for family time, because spending time with loved ones is important to me.

As 2016 progressed, word of my mentoring continued to spread. It didn't take long before I had all 10 groups contracted for 2017! I continue to test and tweak, and, quite frankly, I think I'll be doing that for the remainder of my career.

The beginning stages of this journey have been quite rewarding. I see reps lap it up, sensing opportunities to implement strategies they've never heard, using tools to overcome insurmountable fears.

It's incredibly rewarding waking up each day feeling excited to engage with your work, retaining confidence in your abilities, and reveling in the difference that it will make for the reps who listen and implement the concepts you have so passionately developed with them.

I'm anxiously awaiting the second stage of my business, which will bring a scalable model to my mastery program in order to touch people all over the world and help them tap into their God-given potential.

But at the same time, even with the unlimited market in our country, few reps tap into their full potential in this business. Let's face it, when you're firing on all cylinders as a financial advisor, you're performing a service that matters, as well as having a positive impact on your clients' lives. You're in control of your career, set your own hours, and are free from having a boss who limits your income. You set whatever amount of achievement you're willing to achieve.

It doesn't get any better than that.

Yet so few people live the good life in this industry. To them, it's a grind. It comes with the daily stress of figuring out how to pay their bills or having enough potential clients to talk to. They are only as good as their most recent sale.

That is not how it should be.

I'm committed to succeeding in this journey through my experience as a financial representative, coupled with my experience of developing reps to an elite level, all fired by my passion. I remain excited about using the *Sales Cycle Mastery* program to impact the lives of thousands of reps, by teaching these reps how they can help their clients and themselves prosper as never before.

BRIDGE YOUR GAP • JIM EFFNER

BRIDGE YOUR GAP • JIM EFFNER

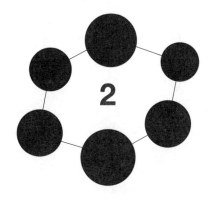

MY HEARING LOSS

It was September 2001, as I attended my office's annual compliance meeting, which every licensed financial rep must endure to fulfill federal compliance and supervision requirements. As you may imagine, it's not a very exciting meeting, probably the most dreaded of the year for financial reps.

About an hour into the meeting, a bad headache suddenly hit me. Quite frankly, I chalked it up to the meeting's dreary subject matter and to my bad mood in general that day. As time passed, my headache intensified. I had never experienced a migraine headache prior to that, but I assumed that's what this was.

Three hours in, it reached a point where my head ached so profoundly that I knew I would have to walk out. It was a tough choice, simply because failing to fulfill the entire four hours requires starting over and taking another class! But I was in so much pain I had no choice. I begged off, stopped at a 7-Eleven for Excedrin migraine medicine, and returned to my office. Our office health club staffed a masseuse who happened to have an opening when I arrived. She massaged my scalp, which I hoped, along with the medicine, would alleviate my headache.

I drove home in somewhat of a blur after the massage. I made it home and slumped into a family room lounge chair for a couple of hours.

My wife came in and took one look at me. "What's wrong?"

I told her and she put a cold compress on my forehead, but the pain only increased. Somewhat coincidently, an old college friend happened to call my wife at this moment. My wife explained my symptoms.

"He's in a great deal of pain," my wife said into the phone. Then she listened a moment, turned to me and asked, "Do you have any problems moving your neck?"

I hadn't noticed any neck issues until that point and I just shrugged.

My wife yelled out, "Jim, can you move your neck?"

I realized I couldn't.

My wife hung up the phone and told me that my friend had another friend experiencing the same symptoms and was diagnosed with meningitis.

Just the word struck fear into me. My health had always been robust, and I was young, too young for a serious illness, I thought. But I remembered stories from my childhood of people with meningitis dying or being left paralyzed. After a moment of panic, my wife and I assured each other that it was probably something else, but we hurried to the car and immediately drove to the emergency room.

At the emergency room, I was in more pain than ever before, or since. My head felt as if it might explode. The ER staff gave me pain medicine, but no matter how much they administered, the pain persisted. Unable to diagnose the problem, they said they needed to run a CAT scan.

I had never experienced a CAT scan. As you may know, technicians slide patients into a huge electronic tube, a kind of X-ray. Though I was not typically claustrophobic, I wasn't in any hurry to get inside the contraption. I was told to remove my wedding ring, watch, and anything metallic. They hooked up an I.V., telling me that whatever they were shooting into my veins would help them see my insides better. I laid down on the attached table, at 6'6" barely able to keep my feet aboard. Then the CAT scan whirred and whined, and I was lifted up and slipped inside. The tech spoke to me as she worked, telling me from time to time to hold still, though I didn't realize I was squirming.

The whole thing took 10 minutes or so, and, while I don't want to discourage or scare anyone away from getting this vital scan when its needed, I found the experience tense and unnerving, as the confining, noisy machine only magnified my fears that I had contracted viral meningitis.

Finally, the tech announced over the CAT scan speaker, "Done! Let's get you out of there."

Then, it was time to wait. My wife and I were told it would take up to a few hours. Every minute seemed to tick by in slow motion before the doctor came back to speak to us. I sat on an examining table; my wife stood at my side.

Yes, he said soberly, it was meningitis.

I saw my wife slump. And while I didn't exactly see my entire life flash before my eyes, I did see the faces of my parents and my kids, and other times in my life, before I managed to suck in a deep breath and settle myself down a bit.

Meningitis. The word just kept replaying in my head. There are words that strike dread in our souls – cancer, the plague, and, for me at least, meningitis was one of those words.

The doctor told us that two other patients in the hospital had also been diagnosed with meningitis that day, the first cases of meningitis in that hospital for nearly five years. Misery may love company, but that didn't make me feel any better.

The doctors told me that meningitis strikes people in waves in various geographic areas. To this day, we don't know how I contracted the disease, but they theorized that I was exposed to West Nile virus, transmitted through a mosquito bite, which can lead to meningitis.

I don't remember much of that day due to the pain

medicine. I spent the night in the hospital and woke up the next morning feeling slightly improved but still heavily medicated. By the following afternoon, the pain had subsided, enough so that they felt comfortable sending me home. Other than controlling my pain, they said they could do little else to help me. We just had to wait and hope and pray. I could see that the doctor felt helpless. He wasn't the only one.

I stayed in bed for two more days until, feeling normal again, I returned to work Friday morning to catch up. I really thought I had dodged a bullet. Here I had contracted one of the most potentially lethal diseases and, although I had intense pain for three days, I basically came out okay. Or at least I thought.

That weekend, Lynn and I had plans with the kids. I was determined to go through with them, especially now, in case I might not be able to in the future. At that point, our oldest daughter, Brittney, was five, Briana three, and Bryce two. We had booked a hotel room at the downtown Chicago Four Seasons for both Friday and Saturday nights. We had a wonderful evening as a family on Friday night, and on Saturday we walked the streets of Michigan Avenue. Later that afternoon, we enjoyed dinner at the Cheesecake Factory. I had purchased tickets to Beauty and the Beast, Disney's ice-skating extravaganza at the United Center. Little did I know when I entered the stadium that that would be the last time I would hear anything for the rest of my life without the aid of modern electronics.

We watched a wonderful musical. The kids and Lynn and I had a blast. Then it ended and we filed out with the crowd. Then, suddenly, while walking up the United Center stairs, the world suddenly went silent around me. For just a second, the word *meningitis* entered my mind, but I quickly dismissed it. This was a hearing issue, nothing to do with meningitis! I didn't put two and two together connecting my hearing loss to the meningitis. I had no reason to. I simply thought I had a head cold and clogged ears.

Now I must explain that I had had a bout of swimmer's ear in the fourth grade, which had considerably compromised the hearing in my left ear, leaving me with about 95% hearing loss in that ear. So, it was not unusual for me to experience a nearly complete hearing loss when my right ear was affected by head colds and congestion. Aside from the fact that I had been exposed to meningitis, this experience didn't feel a whole lot different than what I had already experienced any number of times before.

After taking a taxi back to the Four Seasons, that night turned into the longest of my life. As my wife and kids slept, I stared at the ceiling into the wee hours, wondering if the meningitis had endangered my hearing, as well as my life.

The following morning, a Sunday, I drove home still unable to hear anything. I dropped my wife off with the three kids, drove myself to the emergency room, and immediately called my brother Bob to tell him what had happened. He soon met me in the emergency room.

It's quite an interesting and frustrating experience when you have a traumatic event and medical professionals really can't do anything about it. In some ways, they treated it as no big deal. The ER physician examined my ears, nose, and mouth, and essentially concluded he could do nothing, that the hearing loss was most likely an after-effect of the meningitis. Hopefully, he explained, time would eventually bring my hearing back.

He sent me home with nothing – no real hope, no medicine – saying, "You need to see an ENT specialist on Monday morning when the offices open up. Here's somebody I recommend."

I left with no solid hope for recovery, just the doctor's business card and a great deal of frustration and anxiety.

That Monday morning, I immediately scheduled an appointment with an ENT that afternoon. The ENT told me that my hearing loss definitely resulted from the viral meningitis. The infection had damaged the nerve endings of my inner right ear, causing complete deafness in that ear. Coupled with the near-deafness I already had in my left ear from childhood meant I was in big trouble. He explained that sometimes inner ear nerve endings come back after the inflammation recedes, but sometimes they don't. They could come back in as little as an hour or take as long as six months. He added that the highest probability would be hearing recovery within the first 30 days, but if not, the chances of my ever hearing again were slim to nil.

He then referred me to an advanced specialist who could potentially increase the probability of my nerves returning to normal function. That's when I met Dr. Batista. He said the next step would involve injectable steroids, since the original ENT gave me oral steroids, which failed to work. He recommended three doses of injectable steroids once a week for three weeks, and we got started.

During the treatment process, you sit in a chair as the medical team secures a wire cage around your head, pivoting it so that the one ear points to the ground, the other ear to the ceiling. Next, they slide a very long needle into your ear and inside your eardrum. Yes, it's intensely painful, but it's also imperative that you don't move for 30 minutes while the steroids go to work.

After completing the first injection, the doctor set a timer and left the room. It was four walls and just me. I had that half hour to contemplate that if the three injections failed, I probably had no hope to hear again.

I remember that session as if it were yesterday. Every troubling thought and emotion imaginable churns through your head when you're totally deaf, completely immobilized, and cannot do anything but think. The most intense feeling that I experienced was total and complete loneliness.

Shortly after the first injection, all my time shifted to prayer: quiet conversation with God. I'd always been a man of faith, but I'm almost certain that this incident truly put my faith to the test and, quite frankly, strengthened it. My conversations with God involved turning my future over to Him and asking His will to be done and telling Him that that if I could ever hear again, I wanted to share my experience for the benefit of others in whatever way He saw fit. If I could be an example of overcoming adversity, individual strength, and a mentor to others going through tough times, then they could see me as somebody with whom they could relate. I wanted to be there for His purpose and for His plan. Little did I realize what He had in store for me.

I remember during those three sessions every emotion that raced through my mind. The first, most predominant feeling was fear; if I couldn't do my job because I couldn't hear, then I could no longer provide for my family. It was at that point that my very real fear led to very real anxiety, even slight depression. The news got worse; by the end of the third injection, I had to come to terms with the fact that the treatment was not going to work.

Three other significant things happened in September 2001. The first became one of the most celebrated days of my professional career; on September 1 of 2001, I was appointed managing partner of a Northwestern Mutual network office at age 34, one of the youngest managing partners in company history. This marked the pinnacle of my career and, at such a young age, a cause for celebration.

Then, 10 days later came one of the most destructive days in United States history when the towers were struck down in New York City on September 11th.

The third event occurred when my father suddenly fell violently ill during the last few days of September. He passed away in early October. My dad and I were close, so his loss hit me hard. I really wanted him to enjoy my promotion as a managing partner. I knew that I had made him proud, and I looked forward to the journey together. I also wanted to see him continue to enjoy our children as "Grandpa."

So, on top of the managing partner promotion, the terrorists' attack, and my father's passing, I now had to deal with being deaf. Believe me, there were times when I felt this was all too much for me to handle.

At this time, though, I learned that I had a fantastic staff. I met with my longtime assistant, Margaret, and a newly appointed assistant, Lori. With my wife by my side, I informed them about my health issues and assured them that together we would get through this. We called Bill Beckley, head of our distribution system and the managing partner who happened to recruit me into the business in 1989. I urged my wife to tell him I had a plan and to please be patient as things were going to be okay. Bill's only concerns were on how my wife, Lynn, and I were doing. He expressed zero concern about business – a testament to his remarkable character and his confidence in me. His support meant a lot to me.

Then, finally, I found a ray of hope. The doctors said that I was a perfect candidate for a procedure known as a cochlear implant, or implanting electronic devices in my ear canals, which might allow me to hear if all went well.

The doctors told me that they could not do a cochlear implant hearing device until six months after the onset of hearing loss in to order determine if a chance of natural recovery is low enough for surgery. You see, when they perform cochlear implant surgery, they excise your natural inner ear, so you'll never be able to hear naturally again. Of course, they don't want to do that until they feel there's clearly no chance of recovery without the surgery.

As with most surgery, there were a number of possibly serious complications (surprising to me was that meningitis was one of the risks of surgery!), and there was no guarantee of success. But clearly this was my best option for regaining my hearing. No way I was not gonna go for it!

I'll never forget the interesting day in April 2002 when I admitted myself for cochlear implant surgery. From my first hearing loss before rushing to the emergency room, I always hoped to get my hearing back. And with each successive treatment option that failed, another treatment option always existed. But the cochlear implant was the last chance. Dr. Batista informed me that the cochlear implant at that point only worked roughly 60 to 65% of the time, so I had no guarantees.

However, the definition of "working" involves varying degrees. Working for some people means they can barely hear. Working for others means they can hear and function in the normal world. In other words, despite a 65% success rate for cochlear implants, I faced a high probability that it would not work well enough to lead a fairly normal life.

After the surgery, the implant was still not completely attached, because they don't connect it until the scar tissue on the outside of your head heals, the stitches are removed, and the swelling subsides. I remember coming out of surgery with my head wrapped as if I'd been mummified. I asked my wife to take a picture in anticipation of giving a speech in the future and blowing away the crowd with images from my experience. I wanted to honor the promise I made to God that if He returned my hearing, I would be an example to others. (Of course, I saved the "mummy" picture.)

Approximately two weeks after surgery, I visited my audiologist. Looking back, I don't know why I went alone, but when you have young children you do what you must. Lynn had her hands full and there was virtually nothing she or anyone could do, so I went to the audiologist by myself. My thoughts raced and my nerves were on edge that morning driving to the appointment that would connect and turn on my cochlear implant.

The moment of truth had arrived. It took roughly 30 minutes for the audiologist to connect the device via a magnet that had been placed inside my skull during surgery, and this, I was told, would be followed by an hour of fine tuning. I thought this meant that the pitch might be a little too high or too low and it would need to be "tuned" – kind of like tuning a piano in that it would still create sound but would need tuning to be as accurate as possible.

The moment they turned on the implant, I experienced the greatest fear since first losing my hearing. Then, what I did hear led to me believe the whole thing had been a failure.

Imagine listening to a television and turning the volume

all the way up, but only hearing a loud "static" sound. That's all I heard! At that point that I felt the greatest sense of depression I'd ever encountered. I thought it was over, that it had failed. My physician did her best to encourage me and let me know that the effectiveness of the implant might improve with time.

Then they sent me home. Alone behind the wheel, more alone than I'd ever felt, I cried the entire journey. My last hopes had been dashed. I was crushed.

But even though I knew I faced a challenging future, I didn't feel that I should let Lynn see my fear. I mustered my courage and put on my best poker face before walking in the door. I did the best I could to look normal, but Lynn realized I couldn't hear and this deeply saddened her.

The day dragged on. Then – I don't remember the exact time – in the early afternoon, God's magic started to work. There's really no explanation other than that.

Lying in my bed that night with my cochlear still turned on, the TV flickering away in front of me, I suddenly realized that I could hear it. I could understand the sounds coming from the television for first time in six months!

Lynn was in the walk-in closet of another room. I shouted to her, "Hon, I think I can hear now!"

She muttered something encouraging, her tone indicating that she remained sadly unconvinced. I told her to say something, I forget what, but I repeated it verbatim. She darted around the corner, wide-eyed and joyous.

My cochlear implant worked, and the rest of my future looked bright.

That's the story of losing my hearing and experiencing the fear of wondering if I would ever function normally again. I felt like a cancer patient who goes through chemo, becomes cancer-free, and returns to a normal lifestyle.

Of course, although my cochlear worked, my life was never the same again. Almost nobody in my world knows what it's like to be deaf, and my experience with the cochlear implant comes with a lot of intentionality on my part – I prefer to act and live as normally as possible without calling attention to my disability. (I imagine a therapist would tell me that I'm averse to showing weakness.)

But I choose to look at it a different way. I don't ever want others to view me as disabled. I want to fit in and be normal like everyone else. I don't want people to feel sorry for me or have any kind of forced empathy. I think that's pretty much the mentality of every disabled person; they desperately want to fit in with the normal world, and they want others to view them in the same way as everybody else. But the truth of the matter is, I *am* disabled. I am today, I will be tomorrow, and I will be for the rest of my life. Quite frankly, as I write this book, this is the first time that I've ever admitted that.

I cannot tell you the exact percentage of what I hear today. If I had to take an educated guess, I probably hear roughly a third of spoken words, whether communicating with others, watching TV, or whatever. But you learn to cope. When you don't have a disability, you tend to see people missing an arm or a leg or a hand, and you wonder how they function. Yet, people with disabilities figure it out, as I figured out how to deal with my hearing issues.

I put all things into context; if I can't limit the field of topics that an individual is talking about, I only hear 33% of their words. However, if I know the conceptual topic and can keep the conversation on topic, I can connect the dots. But if someone throws a curveball at me, things can get murky. For example, if someone is talking to me about the Chicago Bears, and then they suddenly say, "Boy, did you hear the crack of thunder?" – I would have no idea what they said.

When I watch TV, I might hear a third of the spoken words. When I watch sports or the news, I have fewer problems. And if I'm in the front seat of a car, being able to hear somebody sitting in the backseat is a challenge. When watching a movie, it's usually almost impossible to understand what's going on. Most movies are hard for people to comprehend when they hear 100% of the audio. Imagine hearing only a third of it.

I can tell you about the challenges for someone who is deaf and has a cochlear implant, but I can also tell you that I feel incredibly blessed. I truly believe that the heart of this story is not what I've told you so far – the real story is how I believe everything happens for a reason. The cochlear implant helped build my character and understand how much more I had to change and grow to be the father, the husband, and the man God intended me to be.

I truly believe hearing loss also gave me an enormous

responsibility that I view as a gift. The purpose, I believe, is that God wanted me to serve as an example to others who are struggling in any aspect of life. Through interactions with me, others can learn that hope exists and that there's always light at the end of the tunnel.

I'd like to think I've been an example to many already, but my daily hope and prayer is that I continue to be an example to many over the course of my life.

For those reading this who have been through significant adversity, I would emphasize that God does not give you challenges that you can't handle. I know that if I can handle deafness and the cochlear implant process, there is virtually nothing else in my life that I can't overcome. Having said that, the death of my wife or my child would be a completely different level of challenge, so I'll exclude those – but other than that, I can't imagine adversity more difficult than going deaf as I did.

There are many other interesting aspects of the cochlear implant. For those who have seen one, you know from an aesthetic standpoint that it really stands out. Although the medical advancements over the years have been notable, I appear to have a substantial-sized magnet on the back of my head, in addition to my 6'6" frame. It's always interesting seeing the looks I get from people. I feel as though the stares have lessened over the last 16 years, probably because there have been a steadily increasing number of cochlear implant recipients, and many people have seen them. Early on, however, when I stepped into elevators with reflective doors I always chuckled from seeing someone behind me stare at the back of my head in puzzlement.

Recent cochlear implant advancements have been dramatic in terms of reduced size and improved dependability. Unfortunately, the sound quality has not improved, and I doubt it will improve in my lifetime. When I first received an implant, I had the magnet on the back of my head and cord connected to a hook on my ear. The cord snaked down my shirt and connected to a computer pack on my belt. I used that for a little over a year, before moving to a BTE, which stands for "behind the ear." This eliminated the belt computer and cord up my shirt. Since then, they've added Bluetooth, meaning I can attach it to my cell phone. In addition, they've made them much more water-resistant, so they don't fizzle out if I'm sweating or am caught in the rain. Those are all great improvements and I am forever thankful.

As technology continues to improve, I don't really know where my hearing functionality will go. But I'm sure God will lead me down that path. I've reached out to the cochlear implant manufacturer, to no avail. I would love to be a national spokesman for them. I see very few cochlear implant patients who are truly thriving. I feel sad for those who get a cochlear implant and clearly feel uncomfortable that others view them as disabled. Rush Limbaugh, the famous syndicated radio host, has put cochlear on the map, and his high-profile use of the device may help other implant recipients feel less isolated. I believe individuals with cochlear implants can lead normal lives and continue to conquer their dreams and realize their visions and goals, but they need encouragement. They need to see somebody excelling despite the challenge, and I would love to fulfill that role to the extent that it's meant to be. I remain hopeful that this will happen.

I'm forever thankful to the team I had when I made managing partner – those wonderful and understanding people stayed with me during those first six months of hearing loss. I'm forever thankful for my family and for the friends who treat me normally and include me in their activities, even though they may have to repeat themselves. I'm certain it can be frustrating! I hope I've continued to inspire them and others and that I will continue to lead a life of overcoming adversity, setting a successful example, and demonstrating the strength that comes from hope, strong faith, and understanding that everything happens for a reason.

BRIDGE YOUR GAP • JIM EFFNER

BRIDGE YOUR GAP • JIM EFFNER

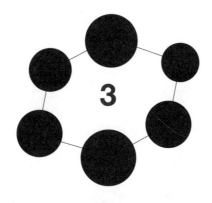

A NEW BEGINNING

In the opening chapter, I detailed my 27-year career in the financial services industry. What I omitted from that story is that I did not choose to leave the last company I worked for. I was terminated and forced to step down as managing partner.

This part of the story is important because, despite the ominous sound of termination, my experience carries so many positive, encouraging messages. I had nothing but success as a financial representative at the highest level, to the point that I reached the top one-half of 1% of the industry in production at a very young age. This achievement led to all kinds of personal growth opportunities, guiding me to the pinnacle of company leadership: a managing partner running an entire network office. The network office that I led consisted of 115 reps, or roughly 400 employees including staff and assistants. I was afforded that opportunity at age 34, making me one of the youngest managing partners in company history.

From childhood, I have been extremely successful at anything I did. My success continued after graduating from college. I was always respected, admired, and viewed in a very positive light, to the point that I accepted the job of managing partner. I often viewed this position as similar to that of an NFL head coach. It comes with a lot of glamour, immense responsibility, and tremendous financial rewards, but, at the same time, it's not a matter of if you'll get fired, it's a matter of *when*.

Although I probably did not want to admit it at the time, it's clear in retrospect that I was stressed out. In fact, I felt somewhat miserable in the last five years at the company. Never in my life had I failed to accomplish and exceed job expectations at the highest levels. Yet this kind of "leadership" job did not align with my passion and skill sets: those of a rep and a trainer. In short, I felt I had moved from company superstar as a rep and trainer to company underperformer as an office manager.

I struggled in that position for two reasons. The first reason was my ego, my pride. It's amazing how self-image can fragment in a very short time. It was difficult for me to occupy a space where I was not one of the top performers, and I failed to manage that difficulty, suffering from self-induced stress, anxiety, and other unhealthy behaviors. In addition to a bruised pride, I also had a tremendous amount of fear. What would happen if I got fired? I had a wife and three kids. I had a plush lifestyle. I was still only in my 40s!

If the worst happened, I would have to swallow my pride. I'd be known as an individual who got fired. I'd have to totally change my lifestyle. I couldn't bear the thought of any of this. (In hindsight, it was myopic and unrealistic, fearing my job prospects would be nil, or that if I got fired, my life would be over.)

During this time of many tense calls from the corporate office, my fear of termination reached an unbearable point, becoming the greatest fear in life.

Then, finally, I received a phone call in February 2015.

"Hey Jim, the head of distribution wants to meet you, but just so you don't start freaking out, he's not going to ask for the keys and have you walk. We just need to have a conversation."

Although his words were not a blatant lie, it wasn't 100% true either, as you'll see.

No more than five minutes into that meeting, my boss told me he no longer believed in me and had decided to make a change. He added that the reason for deceiving me earlier was – based on the amount of integrity I had and how much they could trust me – they wanted me to stick around for four months until finding my successor to make a smooth transition. The company had *never taken this approach prior to me* due to the threat of managing partners aligning with other carriers to take reps with them. A managing partner continuing in this leadership role while awaiting termination could inflict too much damage.

I don't know why they felt sure I wouldn't take another job in the meantime and bring reps with me. I knew I wouldn't do that, but their trust in me was complete and, as it turned out, well founded. I didn't have a single conversation with reps about moving them out of the company.

I must confess that I had the strangest feeling from the moment that they told me I was being terminated. I processed it for about 30 seconds, a tear running down my cheek. At first, I felt sad and scared, and a feeling of desperation lasted until the end of the meeting.

But then something unexpected, even monumental, happened after leaving the office. The moment I slid into my car seat, I felt a huge surge of relief! Never in a million years would I imagine feeling pure relief after being terminated – as if a 500-pound gorilla had jumped off my shoulders after hanging there for five years. It was a surreal and completely unexpected feeling.

I had no idea what I was going to do, but I knew for certain that I would have never left on my own. I had too much pride and a highly competitive nature. Without the company asking me to leave, it would have never occurred.

The company asked me to not discuss my termination until they felt prepared to go public with it. Even 45 days later, nobody in my organization, not even my inner circle of friends – in fact nobody other than my spouse – knew it had happened. But once the news had spread throughout the organization, executive recruiters and other companies quickly bombarded me with phone calls seeking to hire me.

Soon, I had many generous offers for identical jobs with a different company name on my business card. Eventually, I pulled back and refused to have any more employment conversations. I committed to taking a three-month break from any discussions about my career.

I own a lake house, and I fished often during those three months. Obviously, I also reflected on my life and career quite a bit and soon found absolute clarity about one area, even though I didn't yet know what trajectory my career would take. I knew that I never wanted to be in that same situation again – "that situation" amounting to two things: first, not being able to control my destiny; and second, being forced to do something not in alignment with what I'm good at and love doing.

So, that time of reflection centered on looking back at my life for the last 27 years, what I had been doing, when I had been doing it. I realized that I possessed a deep passion for training reps and was uniquely gifted at it. Of equal importance, I realized that my work in that regard mattered and made a difference.

So, as I began to process and plan the next career chapter of my life, I realized that whatever I chose had to center around my passion and talents – the factors I could control. If I accepted a managing partner position at another company, even one with substantial money and abundant opportunities, it would only be a matter of time until I would no longer be in control of my destiny, despite assurances to the contrary. Once, again, I'd be doing things that were not in my wheelhouse. Ultimately, I declined all those opportunities.

As I processed my thoughts, two personal requirements (in addition to self-direction) kept coming back to me as clear as day: teaching sales skills to financial representatives and speaking to large groups. I'm adept at and love both of those things. I knew that thousands of people in the industry needed help. And again, I knew that my work would matter. Even though it came with no guarantees, I decided to build my own company, control my own destiny, and never do anything that didn't fit those two personal requirements, regardless of how much money was involved.

That was the genesis of the P2P Group.

Tremendous challenges came with starting and running the P2P Group after my termination. But I can say that from the start I've never been happier. I feel as if I added five years to my life, and every day I get to do what I love.

Another wonderful aspect of starting my own enterprise: it allows me to dream big. It allows me to embrace the vision of what I want this company to become and the impact I want it to have.

That's not all. I enjoy the daily intellectual stimulation of product development, coming up with new and innovative ideas for delivering my skill set to the industry.

Best of all, my work has a positive impact by helping reps lead a more abundant lifestyle as they significantly impact families and their communities. All of this ultimately drives financial security for those families, so I know my work matters.

The irony is that my economic rewards with this new company are far greater than they may have been had I stayed in my past role, even with as much money as I earned there. Isn't that funny? This was the very thing that I had lost sleep over, probably had high blood pressure over, and had all kinds of stress, anxiety, and fear about!

And because it happened, my health and attitude have improved, my future is brighter, my economic potential is far greater, and every day I'm doing what I love. Isn't that ironic? If you're a man or woman of faith, events have a reason and have a purpose, although often when they happen you don't understand those reasons. If you have the faith and you believe, you can use the events of your life to help create the life you want. This story is about doing that.

I am certainly not trying to boast. I'm simply sharing my story to help others. In looking back, the easy road – the one where you perceive that there are more guarantees and stability – is not always the best route when you reach that proverbial fork in the road. When I started this business, I knew it could be a couple of years before reaching a significant income level. Plus, I had to invest quite a bit of capital to build it. Had I chosen the easy road – a job with a different company – I could have avoided the uncertainty and financial risk of launching my own business. Yet, you only get one life, and if failure is not an option, you do what it takes to succeed. I committed to achieving success.

Nearly everybody I know who was terminated – not

only at my former company but at other companies – simply parked their cars in different parking lots and carried new company business cards with the same job titles. They made this choice because it seemed the easiest, lowest-risk option.

I am proud I took the risk of venturing out on my own. By doing so, I feel that I lead by example. Most important, I can assure my kids that if you set your mind on something, believe in yourself, and work hard, the world is your oyster.

Other important rewards came with my choice. My overall wellbeing and mindset dramatically improved. And the number of people I now impact and touch is exciting, and far greater than I ever imagined. I started this business with the vision that I would work with 10 groups a year for an entire year, a half-day each month for each group. In addition, I would do a few dozen public speaking engagements to various companies and industry associations. That was my business model. That was my big-game vision only two years ago. Boy, has that evolved!

Today we have a burgeoning webpage and an expansive online vision. We intend to take my entire curriculum – including my terminology, hard-earned wisdom and experience, thoughts around mindset, and all of my encouragement and coaching techniques – and create the single-most powerful sales-professional website in the world, specifically catering to the financial services industry. Of course, this website is globally available, allowing hundreds of thousands of people to access my material. And we hope to distribute this book to hundreds of thousands more. This all means that I can help countless more people than I could have impacted by teaching live or delivering speeches to live audiences. An online presence provides an opportunity to create a far greater legacy than if I'd stayed with my old company.

On a personal note, my faith has given me the perspective that God knew where I needed to be, and where I didn't need to be. Although I didn't see it at the time, He gave me strength to trust in Him to follow my passion and to know that He would always guide and lead me, and He has with great abundance.

I hope for those reading this who feel you might be at a low point in your life, that you are in fact on the cusp of something incredibly fulfilling and profitable. I want you to look at it through different lenses and realize that it might just be the genesis of unimaginable growth and an opportunity for a tremendous sense of fulfillment, all there for the taking.

I now have such a positive perspective on life that I never could have found in my old "job." For instance, I learned the truth about who my friends were and were not. The fact is, when you're in a position of authority, you feel as if everybody is in alignment with you and that you have a deep, meaningful, lasting *relationship* with him or her.

That's not necessarily the way it is. Once you lose the title, the position of authority, you may find, as I did, that many people you thought were aligned with you will simply fade away. As the boss, your impact on their future is influential, so these interactions with these individuals generated a sense that a true relationship existed. But when that power is gone, they often go with it. I am blessed to have retained a circle of half a dozen colleagues and friends with meaningful relationships beyond my title. But if you had asked me when I was a managing partner, I would've thought the number of real friends from work was in the forties. When I talk to others who have been in the same situation, they've all experienced some similar circumstances. Your circle is much smaller than you think.

I will wrap up by adding these thoughts: what you do every day creates a reputation, and if you are an individual of integrity and honesty, that reputation never leaves you and will always pay great dividends. At the same time, if you happen to be an individual who doesn't tow that fine line between right and wrong, it will haunt you for the rest of your life.

Fortunately, my reputation is as strong now as ever. I left my former company with dignity and did my best to go out first-class. In my final speech to my organization, I thanked the company for 27 wonderful years. I thanked each colleague for believing in me, and I wished each one the best of luck.

Every day I think about that organization, and I want it to thrive. I want my successor to take what I started and lift it to a higher level. I want the people whom I considered part of my family to enjoy an environment that makes them better, in all ways. I have nothing to prove and nothing to gain by their failures. I don't want them to flounder so that I look better. I want them to thrive, so they can continue to lead the life that I promised when I brought them in. I wish them nothing but the best of luck and a very bright future.

At the same time, I'm now in a different boat, and I want to create the future for my family and my clients, and, in two short years, we are well on the way.

The journey has already been amazing, and the future is bright, exciting, and boundless.

BRIDGE YOUR GAP • JIM EFFNER

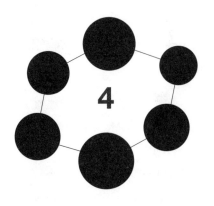

DEVELOPING MY SYSTEM

So when my career of 27 years with the same company that I started with right out of college ended, the next question was what I wanted to do with the next chapter of my life. Within a few weeks of my resignation, I had several companies and executive recruiters reach out to me. Although being "head-hunted" never excited me, I felt as though I owed it to myself to at least listen to their "pitches."

I interviewed with three companies. Two of the recruiters extended an offer very quickly. One realized that he just couldn't afford me, so we went no further. Even though the money was incredibly attractive and similar to what I had been making, I left those meetings sick to my stomach, simply because *it just didn't feel right*. I felt that for this stage of my life, I had the right to be working in my sweet spot. I define my "sweet spot" as what happens when three things come together: 1) only doing what I love to do, 2) only doing what I am exceptionally skilled at doing, and 3) working on a noble path.

It didn't take too long to figure out that I am also gifted at the two things that I love doing: public speaking and sales training. Sales training has always been my strength. It's always been my passion and it's always come naturally to me. I also had the gift of being a "conscious competent," as opposed to an unconscious competent, which meant that I brought *intentionality* to my sales strategies, and I could, therefore, duplicate and teach it. As I figured out that these were the strengths I wanted to put to use going forward, I then had to figure out the environment in which I could do this. When push came to shove, it was also very evident that I never wanted to work for anybody if I wasn't in complete control. I'd always had a desire to be an entrepreneur and to start my own company. Even though there was a great monetary risk to turning away a seven-figure salary (and some fear), the excitement I felt about doing the work I love and excel at signified that going out on my own was the right decision.

What also made my decision easier was that I understood the market opportunity. It didn't take long to figure out there were few full-time professional sales training curricula specifically oriented to the financial services industry that were of any real value. The financial planning industry is massive, and many organizations don't have the infrastructure, systems, or even a process to help their agents become top-level financial sales professionals. This material was desperately needed.

That was it – starting my own company and delivering what I had had in my head for 27 years around sales systems was the plan. How to bring it to life and execute that plan in a way to make a sustainable change was the challenge. Very early on, I knew what I didn't want to do: go on the public speaking circuit and talk briefly to a room full of strangers, delivering merely a motivational speech that had no lasting effect.

I've learned it is impossible to create sustainable change in a one-hour talk, or even a half-day talk. It simply does not work, which meant that once I put all my material together, I needed to figure out how to deliver it in a way that would really create sustainable change. I concluded that I needed to work with people over the course of an entire year.

I knew I needed to bring accountability to my pupils every single month. I decided I would meet with them monthly to reinforce what I had taught the prior month. I also hired coaches that knew my material, my systems, and my processes so they could also work with the sales reps after I left. So, I deliver *Sales Cycle Mastery*, a deliberate live seminar over the course of a year. I travel to a group of reps every month and continue to go back for an entire year. This program has begun to stimulate huge amounts of transformational growth, and I am very proud of the work that we have done.

We have created many ways to distribute these systems to the financial services industry. The most in-depth and personal way is the process I described above, where I work with a group over the course of a year. The second way I can share my story and my process is to write this book, and we hope to distribute it all over the world. The third way is through our website, where people can subscribe on a monthly basis. Here, our subscribers receive every ounce of the knowledge I have accrued over 27 years. The most helpful aspect of these videos and blogs is that it can be accessed in real time and watched repetitively.

I look back at my career in this way: in my 20s and early-30s, I focused on ego and recognition. In my mid-30s to late-40s, I was interested in wealth creation and lifestyle. Now that I'm 50 and entering the fourth quarter of my career, it's all about significance and impact. I created this company with the desire to have a transformational impact on the industry by giving financial advisors the gift of a proven system. When applied, I know this program is transformational and will grow your practice. You can lead a life of abundance. You will deliver a profound amount of financial security to the people in your local community.

But first, you need to understand the Gap!

BRIDGE YOUR GAP • JIM EFFNER

BRIDGE YOUR GAP • JIM EFFNER

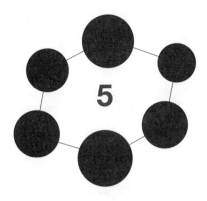

THE GAP – WHAT IS "THE GAP"?

The Gap is the genesis of the P2P Group. It defines both the need and the massive market size for my business model.

Let me describe the Gap. When you break down financial service professionals in the United States, the top 5% make over $200,000 of annually adjusted income. If you do the reverse math, 95% of all financial advisors in the United States earn less than $200,000 a year.

In addition, in my 27 years in this industry, the norm for a financial advisor's month-to-month production is to either barely get by financially or, conversely, produce at a high level. They experience, for the most part, a tremendous inconsistency, generating sales some months and not others. That inconsistency creates tremendous anxiety and damages career passion.

Simply stated, they are leading a secondary life, not coming close to tapping their market potential. I initially witnessed this Gap in 1989, when I first entered the business. I was one of those classic college students, putting minimum effort into my grades and graduating with a mediocre GPA. Many of my fraternity brothers had far superior GPAs, and in practical majors such as engineering and accounting.

When those individuals landed their first jobs out of college, they received "attractive salaries" – what we all thought was a lot of money. For me, not knowing the kind of career or profession to pursue and lacking a favorable GPA limited my job interviews mostly to sales jobs.

Not only did I end up in a sales job, I landed a sales job that paid 100% commission!

I remember it well. In the spring semester of my senior year, at a time when conversations in my fraternity house centered around "What is your starting salary?" and I disclosed I would be working on 100% commission with zero salary, my frat brothers bombarded me with harsh feedback and rounds of laughter. Everyone wanted to know how long it was going to be until I found a "real job."

"Real" came 12 months later when, in my first calendar year of work (1990), I earned in excess of $100,000. All my friends with phenomenal GPAs earned about *half that*.

More important, I loved my job. I had no boss, my future was incredibly bright, and I was in control. Conversely, all my frat friends were miserable; they disliked their jobs, saw no clear path upward, and felt underpaid and unable to do anything about it. I think you can see where I'm going.

So, I'm strutting around the halls of my office at a very young age, thinking *somebody pinch me because this career is awesome*, and baffled as to why everybody wouldn't want to do this. There was no downside to it.

But then I noticed the revolving door of reps coming in and failing, and I realized that the majority of reps led mediocre lifestyles, at best. I didn't understand why, and for the first time I started talking about "the Gap."

What exactly is the "Gap"? The Gap is the vast chasm between the average earnings of most reps and their potential earnings. The fact is that most reps could be earning 2, 3, 4 times what they currently earn – or more. And they could do this working the same hours they work now. How? That's what you'll learn in the following sections of this book.

When you look at the United States savings rate, you'll find that most people save very little. Our country is the world's most affluent, yet we live in a very consumptive society. The highest percentage I've seen of adjusted gross income that the average American saves is 3%. Study after study suggests that individuals need to save somewhere between 15 and 20% of their income to achieve financial security at retirement.

Again, the average American saves 3%, and they need to save 15 to 20%. That tells you there is an enormous opportunity out there. Multiple other studies suggest that the average household with an income of $100,000 or more in the United States only has 1.5 times their earned income in life insurance. Study after study recommends between 10 and 15 times. So, there's another huge area of opportunity.

Let's examine another category: the percentage of people who have an actual financial plan, a working document that defines where an individual is in their life, compared to where they need to be in the critical areas of long-term planning, retirement, college education planning, asset allocation, risk management, and so on.

The percentage of Americans who actually have a plan, and can produce it and show it to you, is *less than 1%*.

And finally, ask what percentage of Americans have a financial advisor who not only produces a plan for their client, but annually meets with the client over a prolonged period, and you're looking at another pathetically low percentage.

When we analyze those stats, they support my point about the Gap. If you're in the financial services industry and your goal is to get people to save more money, buy more insurance, and have an actual financial plan, there is a vast market opportunity. There are countless people you could be talking to. You can call on 15 people a day for the next 50 years and never run out of people to talk to and people to help.

Finally, I want to add that today's technology means your opportunities are unlimited. Not long ago, if you lived in rural America, your opportunities were limited by the scope of your market size. But with today's technology, you can reach nearly everyone, making a very good living helping people who are financially unstable in nearly every corner of the country.

This "Gap" is the genesis of my company; hence, the name, the P2P Group. The P2P approach means taking your unrealized *Potential* and turning it into realized, breathtaking *Performance*.

There you have it. This Gap is enormous, and it defines where the average financial advisors perform compared to their actual potential.

We may sit back and ask, *"Why is that?"* I could write an entire book on just that one question.

We could make the argument that this is not a logical business; rather, it's an emotional business, and one with few individuals who can work effectively in an emotional space where they must master the art of building relationships while dealing with constant rejection. I agree with that assessment.

Of course, the majority of the population isn't employed as financial advisors; this business is for a very select few. Of all Americans, far less than one-half of 1% is employed in this business. So, why can't most of those reps who have qualified and trained for this job thrive?

There probably are four or five primary reasons, but my company focuses on one: improving the professional sales skills of representatives by getting out of their own emotional way, changing their mindset, and applying systems that have stood the test of time.

Most unsuccessful reps "wing" things on a daily basis. They fail to create a structured environment, they don't operate with intention, they are not consistent from client to client, and they perform based on how they feel in the moment. That formula is a death sentence.

We are emotional creatures. We don't wake up every day with our A+ game, but when we have our A+ game, we perform as high-level communicators. That's why some financial advisors have great months. But when we're down and out emotionally, and we don't have our A+ game, we perform poorly, and that's why we have bad months! Sometimes those bad months become devastating.

So, what is the answer? The answer is to get out of your own way, build structured systems and processes around the way you handle your clients throughout the entire sales cycle, and do it over and over and over and over until it becomes absolute habit. Boxers say, "You fight like you train." In other words, disciplined training helps you overcome your emotions under pressure and assure consistency of performance.

The rationale behind the theory is that repetition is the mother of learning. When we repeat things over and over, we excel at them. Malcolm Gladwell's book *Outliers* stated that until you do something for 10,000 hours, you don't become an expert at it.[1] When you prospect the same way for 10,000 hours, you become a master. The practical results

---

[1] Gladwell, Malcom. *Outliers*. New York: Little, Brown and Company, 2008.

occur when we consistently do things the same way, and those ways are well thought out, structured, and proven. We can achieve consistency in our financial practice, rather than our roller coaster production.

When thinking about building my company, I wanted to be sure that not only was it going to be in line with my skill set and my passion – I knew I could help people – I also wanted to make sure my services had a viable market. I truly believe that I struck gold in all those categories. Learning to be an effective salesperson by working with a methodical system is a strength of mine. Furthermore, it's a personal skill set that I am very passionate about teaching.

I know that when reps learn it, follow it, and implement it on a consistent basis, it will transform their lives, elevating them from riding an emotional and financial roller coaster toward enjoying a stable, abundant lifestyle beyond their wildest dreams.

With this in mind, let's reexamine our theme that there exists a Gap between market size and market penetration. I could work with an enormous number of reps every year and never scratch the surface – so many really need this kind of help, which is the reason I went beyond my seminar training to bring scalability to the marketplace and reach far more financial reps than I could attain in person.

My business focuses on working with 120 advisors per year. I work in 10 groups of 10 reps in the initial stage, then pick the two best groups to go to the second level. Because I can work with only 120 advisors a year, it's difficult to have a significant impact on the industry.

This concept brings into focus the excitement and enthusiasm I have about my vision for this business: bringing live training to an online tutorial business. The process of being in the studio and filming every aspect of the sales cycles described in this book, taking everything that I teach live and sharing it online with the world, brings tremendous scalability to the impact I could have in an industry that I'm so passionate about.

One final thought before we move on, and it's vital that all of us understand it: virtually *anybody can do this.*

This business does not require a unique skill set. It simply requires discipline, a solid work ethic, and the desire to learn how to overcome adversity. You must be able to think big, but once you can tackle those skills, you don't need to be genetically wired for the industry or have any specific God-given talents to prosper. You simply must get out of your own way and follow a system.

Now, compare that to other businesses where you can earn well into the seven and eight figures. You had better be a CEO of a Fortune 500 company, or come out of the best graduate school, or become one of the biggest and brightest corporate leaders in the world. You won't be a surgeon unless you're smart enough to get into med school and handle the intellectual load that comes with that. You can't be a rising lawyer in a big firm if you didn't attend an elite law school. And you're not likely to be on Wall Street or in any of the private equity or investment banking firms without elite credentials.

I feel I have exceeded many of those elite professionals in quality of lifestyle, realizing my total economic potential, making an impact on clients, and a difference in my field. That happened because it was up to me, just like it's up to all of you. Anyone reading this book can do this! This is not a motivational or inspirational speech. I'm simply speaking the truth. Reading this book and following the systems, getting out of your own way, and believing in yourself can lead to an abundant lifestyle through absolute transformational growth.

The opportunity is real, the rewards immeasurable, and the work you do can make a difference in people's lives along the way.

Now that we can conclude that an enormous Gap exists out there – which translates to huge room for growth – it's also important to note that, by delivering the Sales Cycle Mastery system you are about to learn in my book, *it is not easy,* nor will your business automatically explode after reading and applying my lessons.

It is, however, a great start in the right direction and without it, there is little hope. With it, you obtain tremendous hope – but only if you remain steadfastly focused on the discipline necessary to perfect it.

I compare it to an amateur cook getting their hands on a recipe of world-class chef's signature dish. Even with the recipe, it requires time and discipline before their preparation methods result in a dish that rivals the world-class chef's masterpiece. And the process, along with the work, necessary to reach the master chef's level is what will ultimately make the real difference, not just having the recipe.

What would that process to greatness look like? They would cook the dish several times, making slight adjustments and tracking tasting notes with each effort. They might create a focus group of friends and colleagues to sample the dish and provide individual feedback. With that information in hand, they'd go back and tweak various parts of the preparation, down to the finest details, like changing ingredients and amounts. And with each tweak and outcome, they'd take more notes and collect more data.

That's the journey to mastering the dish. Who does that? Honestly, very few. That's a major reason for the Gap. I hope as you read my book that you will gain the passion for the *pursuit of mastery*, not only through the gift of the recipe, but by gaining energy from the new possibilities for your future when you apply the information.

BRIDGE YOUR GAP • JIM EFFNER

BRIDGE YOUR GAP • JIM EFFNER

PHOTOS FROM MY LIFE AND CAREER

This picture is of one of my passions, pheasant hunting, with my three best friends from college. I put this in here because they mean so much to me and we are all still friends. Friends are family you choose and these guys are special. (11/88)

Our wedding picture. The best decision I ever made. The picture includes my parents and my in-laws. I can't imagine better parents. Unfortunately, I lost my dad in 2001, but my mom is still going strong at age 86. My in-laws have been amazing and such a support for Lynn, myself, and the kids. Lynn and I have been so blessed! (10/20/90)

A composite of my name badge and ribbons that my wife saved and my staff presented to me years later. This was from the last year I worked as a full-time rep. I'm proud of those memories. (1/2000)

The cover page article of the Northwestern Mutual periodical announcing my appointment to becoming a general agent at 34 years old. (9/01)

My main platform talk at Northwestern Mutual's annual meeting. This was a bucket list goal. There were 11,500 people in the audience. (7/07)

The family skiing at our condo in Breckenridge. There's nothing better than spending the day on a mountain with family. (2/09)

The family together in Hawaii over Christmas. Our family vacations throughout the years bonded us together. These experiences are far more valuable than anything else I can imagine. (12/11)

My Research Council study group. I am honored to have been a part of this group. The wives were more important than the managing partners. The amount I learned from these guys and the friendships Lynn and I formed from this group were off the charts. I love these people!!! (3/14)

Two of my best friends, Leo & Keith, at the annual Tiger Woods Golf foundation at Pebble Beach, with a couple of cool guys we met, Alonzo Mourning and Pat Perez. (10/14)

My family at our lake house with our dog, Toby. There are no words that could possibly explain how much I cherish my family memories at our lake house. (6/15)

My siblings in Napa Valley. I brought them all together for my 50th birthday celebration. I can not imagine better siblings. Being the youngest, I was tremendously impacted by all of them. (4/17)

Bryce with Head Coach James Franklin of Penn State on our visit, where he received his full scholarship offer. What an exciting moment. Lynn and I are so proud!! (4/17)

A picture from the back of the lake house. Special... need I say more!!! (6/17)

Briana, my middle daughter, in her senior photo. What an awesome person she has become!!! Her mother and I are so proud of her!!! (6/17)

All of our best friends (a few missing) in Norwegian Bay in Green Lake, WI, at our lake house for the Fourth of July. This has become quite the tradition and created awesome memories. Lynn and I have been so blessed with these friends. We love them all and life would not be the same without them. (7/17)

The most recent picture with the man that gave me my start, Bill Beckley, my general agent. One of the most influential men in my life.

Brittney's graduation from SMU in Dallas. We are so proud of her and she is already off to a great start in her career (and off the payroll!!). (5/18)

My beautiful bride and I at Bryce's high school graduation party. She is my rock and my world. Happy marriage = happy life... AMEN!!! (6/18)

Working with a monthly group in New York City delivering my Sales Cycle Mastery *curriculum. These reps are changing their practices and it's so fun to be along for the ride. (2/18)*

Delivering a Prospecting Mastery Workshop. When reps master the art of prospecting, transformational growth occurs in their practice. (4/18)

BRIDGE YOUR GAP • JIM EFFNER

PROSPECTING

We must be aware that the single biggest reason reps fail to grow in this business is a lack of quality people to call on. Unsuccessful reps have an inability to master the art of functioning as a professional prospector. The foundation of working as a master prospector is understanding which leads to pursue and which leads one should not pursue.

But first you need to understand *why*. Why do you need to prospect? And you also need to realize that the answer changes from time to time.

In the beginning, we prospect because we have no choice. We need people to call. But once we have been in the business for a few years and we have enough clients to call on, need gives way to desire – a desire to contact people we look forward to doing business with. At that stage, we can grow our business. If you introduce me to a rep that is in a rut or is bored, I guarantee you that this rep has not mastered prospecting. Reps such as this are bored by the people they work with. They lack the desire and drive to forge relationships with clients. In short, they are not being challenged.

Professional prospecting can pull you out of that rut. You can live your career by design by identifying the people you want to work with – people who are engaging and in the economic markets and careers that you want to work with. Excellent prospecting is a conduit that will enable you to land these clients and reach this point.

The step of setting aside time to determine who you will prospect requires me to explain why it's no longer effective to ask "every" lead or client for a referral.

The fact is, every rep has clients that, for one reason or another, they are not very enthusiastic about. This could be for a host of reasons: they don't earn enough money or have enough assets to manage; they fail to promptly return calls or emails (meaning they probably don't respect their advisor that much); they live so far away from your office that it is simply inefficient to visit them, etc.

I have found that people tend to refer reps *to those friends or colleagues who are much like themselves.* With this in mind, only ask those clients who are the most qualified, who are people you like and get along well with, who you are excited to deal with and help on a day-to-day basis. You want to "clone" these clients, to get more clients like them, not get more of the type of clients who don't make you money or with whom you would rather not spend time. Keep this in mind as you ask for referrals, and the success of your efforts will grow accordingly.

With that in mind, let's establish a true working definition of a "referral."

When defined by someone less than a master prospector, a referral is simply the name of a person. A master prospector, however, knows that a person is a referral only *when someone introduces someone they trust to someone they care about.* This, then, is an individual the client cares enough about to entrust you with their financial well-being. Prospecting is all about influencing a current client to nominate you so that you can get in front of the prospective client on a very favorable basis.

All too often, prospecting in the business is simply broken down to a process of gathering names and pounding the phones. Merely calling prospects is not what I teach. It's not what I'm all about. Getting a name is just the beginning. The art of prospecting is persuading an individual to go out on a limb to introduce you in a very positive, favorable fashion to a qualified person. (NOTE: If you are relatively new to the business, this step does not apply. Until you have made it in this business, you need to ask qualifying questions all the time.)

So, as I alluded to earlier, there's a shift here from your early career, when the purpose for prospecting is to hustle and obtain countless names, to slowing down after your career is well underway, targeting and getting powerful, favorable introductions, even when the raw numbers of prospects are fewer.

Before digging deeper into prospecting, we must also check our financial rep mindset. Most reps struggle with prospecting and carry a self-defeating mindset to their sales approach. They may believe the client is going to have to do them a favor or that they aren't knowledgeable enough so they feel uncomfortable asking for the prospect's business. We require the *right* mindset – an empowering mindset – before dabbling in this kind of prospecting.

First, reps must examine their character, particularly their honesty. Make sure you would never do anything for anybody that you wouldn't do for yourself in the same scenario. A high level of integrity and honesty is incredibly valuable.

Second, reps must understand that they can bring a tremendous amount of value by asking the right questions and engaging the prospect to think about things they have never thought about before. Regardless of whether the prospect becomes a client, the rep still adds enormous value by jumpstarting the client's mental processes in the matter by asking key financial questions.

And remember: the most empowering mindset is that you, as a financial advisor, are presenting your client with an opportunity to give a gift to someone they care about. It's not that the client is doing the financial advisor a favor; in fact, it's quite the opposite. The financial advisor is doing the client a favor by giving them the opportunity to introduce a life-changing relationship.

Once you adopt the proper mindset, initiate the process through understanding that *how you ask for referrals* is important. You also must understand that a mere glib "pitch" will not determine whether your client gives you referrals. Your client will provide referrals based upon the experience and trust they develop with you. Nonetheless, the language you use to ask for referrals can greatly affect your outcome. Choosing the optimum approach can give you confidence to increase the chances of referrals.

Let's examine the prospecting workshop system. There is an eight-step process to becoming a masterful prospector. While all eight steps are important, the first step is crucial.

1) Begin each month knowing how many leads you need and be in tune with where you are *every single day of the month*.

Think about it this way. If you're going on a journey but have no idea where you're going and wander around aimlessly, you're obviously never going to reach your destination. It's the same with prospecting. You need to know the exact number of referrals needed to meet your goal and make your business come alive. For example, if a rep needs 50 referrals in any given month, he or she doesn't only need to meet that monthly goal, but also must have a keen awareness of where he or she stands every single day.

It's like losing weight. Each day, we need to step on the scale to gauge our weight. There are many reasons for using this strategy; the most compelling reason is that knowing where we stand helps us make better daily decisions. It's the same with prospecting. If we ignore our progress or have a wandering goal, we won't hit our referral goals. This is why knowing exactly where you stand every day, and openly communicating this vital information to your staff, tops the list. I recommend this approach for all reps.

It's also crucial to drive home the point that the mentality of "more is better" is unacceptably vague. I have seen countless reps with no idea what their monthly referral goal is due to a mentality of "I'm simply going to try as hard as I can and the more I get, the better." Reps must take time to plan and have a precise idea of their business needs.

Again, reps must be clear about when to actually count a referral as a referral. For example, a rep could use the following definition. *My referral must be with a candidate who is married, has children, earns more than $100K per year, has accurate contact info, and the nominator is willing to provide a favorable introduction.* Upon receiving a referral, if all of those requirements are not met, that name *does not count as a referral.*

With this in mind, if a rep previously received 80 names per month, but many did not earn $100K per year and several others failed to meet various requirements, they may now average fewer leads per month, but those leads will be qualified. The overriding point here is that reps are far better off when prospects meet all of their referral definitions.

Also, share your goals with your leader or partner. When

two or more people know their goal and their progress, they have a much higher likelihood of hitting that goal.

2) Have a process to effectively feed a name that fits into your target market that your nominator knows.

It is not the client's responsibility to come up with a prospect. As a financial advisor, your job is to know whom you want to meet. You also need to be certain that the client knows the prospects well.

With that knowledge in hand, you simply want to feed that name to the client rather than waiting for a referral, which may never materialize. Never look at prospecting as getting a name. Today's increased access to the internet and social media ensure that it is easy to find the name of a desired referral. What you need is for people to nominate you and introduce you in a powerful way, so the ball is already set up on the tee when you call them. That's what prospecting is all about. Going forward, this is the mindset that I want you to adopt.

Your chances are greatly enhanced by identifying prospects you want to meet by researching them ahead of time. You should always bring three or four names to a prospecting meeting. Suggest the names and state, "I know you know this individual, and this is someone I'm really trying to meet. Will you do me a favor and introduce me?"

Your staff should be instrumental in developing a feed list. The last thing I want one of my reps to do is to sit at their computer searching for names. Help your staff become effective at compiling feed lists and confirming prospects of the type you will be excited to meet.

3) Begin every week by looking at your calendar and identifying whom you want to prospect and follow through with it.

Successful reps grow up in the business with the mentality that they must ask for referrals in every meeting. If they don't, they develop an overwhelming sense of guilt.

I recommend sitting down on Wednesday or Thursday to review the upcoming week and identify those you wish to prospect. Give your staff those names and have them provide information on these individuals so you feel prepared.

The other reason we want to do this is to bring intentionality to our prospecting. Often, reps either forget to ask, run out of time, or simply feel uncomfortable about imposing on a client for names. I never want my reps to do anything based solely on what they feel because they will usually make poor decisions.

I want reps to know ahead of time that they are going to prospect with this client. They should be prepared for the prospect, make sure they leave ample time at the end of the meeting to inquire, and then follow through on it.

Think about it as the ultimate accountability on your part. Let's say you give a client name to your staff well in advance, and your staff works hard to prepare a feed list of his or her acquaintances. If you come back to the office and tell them you didn't ask for a referral, their hard work was wasted, and they'll lose any passion for feed list research. I believe this approach builds an awesome level of accountability in a rep's world. Identifying ahead of time the names that a rep plans to ask his client not only makes them more prepared, it ensures that they will follow through.

4) Always have prospecting on your agenda.

The next step is to have prospecting on your agenda every day. Obviously, you would not do this with a brand-new client. However, if you are meeting an existing client for an annual review or a client after completing fact-finding and are working on a plan, begin your meeting with an agenda.

The agenda should list exactly what you want to accomplish in the meeting. At the bottom of the agenda, add networking or prospecting, depending on which word feels more comfortable. Next, simply review the agenda at the beginning of your meeting to obtain permission and buy-in from the client – confirmation that the agenda is on pace with their expectations. Once that is done, proceed with the meeting.

The first benefit is that a client-approved agenda provides a psychological buy-in for prospecting. The second benefit is that you won't forget to prospect if it's on the agenda. Finally, the client may already be thinking about how and who they can help you with when you review that at the very beginning of the meeting.

5) Manage your time efficiently.

This step focuses on efficient time management and making sure you reserve a quality amount – usually 12 to 15 minutes – at the end of the meeting to prospect.

You can improve your performance here by holding meetings in quiet, confidential locations, such as the client's private office or your conference room, rather than in a public setting. You want an environment conducive to getting things done, with very few, if any, distractions.

Of equal importance, remember that you are in charge of the meeting. You are the leader. You set the tone. That attitude keeps you on pace and assures that you're aware of the time. Inform the client at the beginning of the meeting that you're both busy and you want to respect their time. Let them know from the outset when the meeting will end. Setting your watch on the table is a wonderful signal that you respect their time. It also helps them understand that you are very busy, and that is a positive thing.

Finally, we also want to learn how to rein in our clients. When they begin to pontificate about meaningless data, we can get way off base in our timing.

In sum, once you identify a desirable individual for prospecting, being efficient with time is absolutely necessary. The reason this is so critical is that I have found that effective prospecting takes a good 10 to 12 minutes at the end of the meeting. More often than not, reps are rushed at the end and leave 2 to 3 minutes to prospect. That does not work!

6) Refine your language and make it consistent. Overcome fear through verbal repetition.

I constantly work with reps to ensure that they track their language when communicating with prospects.

A rep should tighten his or her language and be able to explain concepts at the drop of a hat in a way that sounds fantastic.

When well versed in the business, reps can think about talking points while maintaining eye contact, smiling, using an appropriate tone and effective inflections, and demonstrating good posture (I understand that 80% of all communication is nonverbal). In fact, once comfortable with discussion tactics, *when you no longer need to think about talking*, you can greatly improve in all nonverbal aspects.

I also believe that when reps can automatically recite the necessary information, they portray a tremendous amount of confidence.

Reps struggle with prospecting for many reasons, the most common being fear. One trigger for fear is discomfort with what you are saying or how you are saying it.

Repetition dissipates this fear. To best achieve verbal repetition, practice with the focus of a professional athlete. I highly recommend using your phone or webcam to record language rehearsals. Recruit your spouse or a friend to offer honest, constructive feedback on your verbal presentation. The goal of these exercises is to master your presentation until you can recite it in your sleep.

7) Develop a smooth, well-crafted response to the top four objections associated with asking for prospects.

This is a critical aspect. Typically, clients are unwilling to give referrals on the first ask and are likely to respond with one of the following:

- I can't think of anybody.
- The person is all set.
- Let me talk to them first.

- I know they already have an investment advisor.

Once you've been in the business for at least six months, you've heard these objections hundreds of times. Reps are continuously thrown off guard when a client offers one of these objections. In my process, you must become very comfortable and very confident in your approach to overcoming them. They are not difficult, but being caught unprepared can throw you off. Use language that makes you comfortable.

Now let's look at solutions to these common objections.

Solution to the second objection: If the individual tells you that their friend is all set, I would simply reply: "Here's what happens when I get out and meet people. I take them through a detailed process, just like I did with you, and what I find is one of two things will happen. The first thing that could happen would be that once I uncover all of the information, I confirm that they have all their i's dotted and their t's crossed. The current advisor is doing a great job in that scenario. I tell them that and they feel much better about the job that their advisor is doing."

I continue to explain: "The second scenario that can happen is where I cover all of their information and I discover gaps and holes in the plan that the current advisor has not made them aware of. When this happens, they are so incredibly happy that they met me because otherwise they would have never found out there was a potential problem. So, the way I see it, Mr. Prospect, either one of those outcomes is positive. Wouldn't you agree? Great. Please tell me the phone number."

Solution to the third objection: When clients claim they want to talk to their friends first, the rep needs to understand that no client can handle getting you in the door better than you can.

Any time a client calls a friend to ask permission for a referral, the answer is almost always no. You don't want that.

Instead, you could suggest, "Hey, listen, I'd love for you to talk to him because it is your prestigious relationship and your influence that's going to get me in. I'll put together an email and send it to you. Then, you can either copy and paste it or forward it over to your friend. That way, he gets the information ahead of time, and then I can follow up with him. I'll wait 48 hours. If he gives you any kind of negative reaction, reach out to me."

Note, however, if the nominator agrees to the email, but receives any kind of negative reaction from the prospect, the rep must say that he or she will NOT call the prospect in an attempt at further communication.

In essence, you're controlling what they're saying to the friend. You're putting it together, yet not exposing the client to a situation where their friends tell them they're not interested.

Solution to the fourth objection: The response to this is almost identical to the second objection. If a client says their friends already have advisors, you simply respond, "I'd be surprised if they didn't have an advisor based on the character and the quality of this individual that you've told me about. Having said that, one of two things happens when I meet with individuals. After I gather all the information around their situation, like I did with you, the first scenario is I just confirm that the advisor that they currently have is doing a great job. When that happens, they feel that much better about their current advisor. The second outcome is where I uncover problems and holes in their plan that their current advisor is not making them aware of. In this scenario, they're very glad they met me because otherwise they never would've known those gaps and holes existed. The way I look at it, Mr. Prospect, either situation is positive. Wouldn't you agree? Great, please tell me their phone number."

Any of these solutions will work, or you can simply create your own. The bottom line: practice smooth deliveries of compelling responses to common objections. You must also convey confidence when stating it, as well as anticipate assumed consent.

Solution to the first objection: Notice I didn't initially explain how to overcome the objection that the client can't think of anybody (you did, right?). This is the most common objection and I'll now teach you how to stop that objection before it even starts!

What do I mean by that? I mean that you never ask for a referral again without feeding the client a name. It isn't the prospect's job to think of someone. It's your job, through research you and your staff have done to identify who you want to meet from that client's circle of friends, family, and associates. If you never again ask an open-ended "Who do you know?" question again, you'll have stopped that objection before it even starts.

Let's say that your research reveals someone your client knows well, someone who he works with, someone who we'll call Billy Smith. When you ask for a referral, it should sound something like this: "I know Billy Smith is a work associate of yours. He sounds like someone I'd like to meet, someone I think I can help. Could you introduce me to him?"

There are two reasons for this approach. First, it completely eliminates the objection that normally comes from asking the wrong way: the "Who do you know?" approach that I've warned you about. (And to which, the client is likely to say he can't think of anyone, and he probably will be telling the truth when he says that.) The second reason to feed the name is that it puts you in charge of who you're potentially going to be talking to, based upon research you've done, not just "someone" that your client happens to think of who may or may not be qualified.

Never stray from this strategic, disciplined approach again, and the number – and the quality – of your referrals will soar!

8) Create a system to process your referrals.

This should be done consistently each time. First, communicate to the nominator exactly what will happen, how it will happen, and when it will happen. Second, you and your staff need to follow through and make sure the process happens each and every time. We can't let referrals stack up in our office until we're not busy. When too much time passes after the nominator says great things, the prospect may have forgotten. We must reach out to these people in a timely fashion.

To most effectively know where you stand every day as it relates to your referral number, I encourage a daily seven-minute stand-up meeting with your staff.

Every morning, address the following questions. What is our referral goal this month? Where do we stand right now in relation to that goal?

This accomplishes a few critically important things. First, it brings a heightened level of awareness to you and your team about where you stand, which has a positive impact on the decisions you make that day about prospecting. Second, it prevents anything from falling through the cracks from a processing perspective. Imagine if you tell your staff that you have 34 referrals month-to-date and they claim they have only received and processed 28 from you. You'll get on the same page quickly with the seven-minute stand-up meeting.

Success in this business requires a high volume of efficient activity every day. If you're all over the board and ineffective about processing referrals, it will slow you down. By consistently delivering as described to your client when you got a referral, you and your staff stay on the same page and process referrals efficiently. Adopting and installing a system to process your referrals is a vital step in becoming a masterful prospector.

I can't stress enough the importance of the "mindset" that I mentioned earlier. You have to believe that you deserve referrals. You have to believe that anyone you meet is an incredibly lucky individual. You have to know that you're always going to do the right thing and that you can help people.

Moreover, you have to believe that people desperately need your help. Instead of thinking your clients are doing you a favor, I want to change that mindset. For the rest of your career, know that you are giving them a significant opportunity. I always taught my reps one example around this mindset: We all know someone who married a person they met on a blind date. Until the day those people die, especially if happily married, they will never forget the person who put them together.

If a financial advisor is sincerely looking to apply for the job of delivering financial security to clients for a 20-,30-, or 40-year journey, I firmly believe that this process will be life-changing for their clients. Those clients will always remember how they originally met their advisor. It truly is an opportunity, and that is empowering.

SYSTEM FOR PROSPECTING

1. Begin each month knowing how many leads you need. Be in tune with your progress towards your goal every single day.

2. Have a process to effectively feed a name that fits into your target market.

3. Begin every week by looking at your calendar and identifying who you want to prospect with. Follow through with it.

4. Always have prospecting on your agenda.

5. Manage your time efficiently in meetings to leave time for prospecting at the end.

6. Refine your language and make it consistent. Overcome fear through verbal repetition.

7. Develop a smooth, well-crafted response to the top four prospecting objections.

8. Create a system to process your referrals.

BRDIGE YOUR GAP • JIM EFFNER

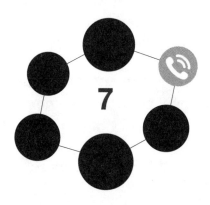

PHONING and CALENDAR MANAGEMENT

As we go into the second step of the sales cycle, we will discuss phoning and calendar management. Like the other steps, it is critically important. I find that, while there is a tremendous amount of training for phoning language and overcoming objections, very few reps are taught *how to manage their calendar appropriately*. Managing our calendar is critically important because time is one of the greatest assets of a rep. If you don't learn how to master calendar management, you'll never reach your full potential.

When working with reps, I always ask them, "Are you in control of your calendar, or is your calendar in control of you?" As with all the concepts I teach, the tools of the trade required to create an efficient calendar are not difficult to figure out on the surface. I think the elephant in the room is often the rep's mentality, rather than a lack of understanding. When it comes to calendar management, I find that reps possess one of two mentalities: the scarcity mentality or the mentality of abundance.

If you have a scarcity mentality, you will never be efficient in calendar management. You must have the mentality of abundance. The theory of abundance is critical.

Let me give you some examples. If you believe you're good enough, that what you do is important, and you operate in a highly populated market, your issue is not to see enough people, but to see the *right* people. You should also adopt the mentality that those fortunate enough to see you are going to be forever thankful you possess an abundance mentality.

If you feel the need talk to anyone who can fog a mirror in order generate the necessary activity to meet your budget and pay your bills, then you have a scarcity mentality. In that case, the first step is changing your mindset. If you have the mentality of abundance, figuring out how to optimize your calendar will be relatively simple. If you have a mentality of scarcity, I encourage you to step outside of your box and try to understand why that is.

Let's move forward, understanding that only those with a mentality of abundance can accomplish this. First, when we look at our calendar, we want to look at why we make appointments. The obvious answer for most is to fill the calendar. However, it's much more than that. We want to fill our calendar with intentionality (purpose). We want the appointment to be the right kind of appointment. We want the prospective or existing client to look forward to the meeting, and we want the appointments to be at the right time, on the right day, and in the right place. When we develop our calendar, this step is critically important. The single most important thing you can do to control your calendar is to learn how to say, "no."

One of my early mentors taught me a lesson that forever stayed with me: his definition of opportunity cost. He explained that every time you say "yes" to something, you are saying "no" to something else. If you agree to meet a potential client who lacks the qualities you want to build your practice around, that costs you time. If it takes 45 minutes to get to that appointment, an hour for the appointment, and another 45 minutes back, you just lost 2 ½ hours simply to keep an appointment with someone you did not want to meet. During that time, you could have conducted market research, identified better potential clients, and made more effective phone calls.

To manage an efficient calendar, we must learn how to say "no" to the wrong kind of appointments (as we discussed in the previous chapter about prospecting). Let's say you have an average client by your standards. That client might be somebody you're willing to see, providing they come to you because of limited time. However, that would definitely be a client you're unwilling to spend a 90-minute round-trip driving to visit. When calling the client, if they refuse to come to you, you must say "no" to the client. If you say "yes," that will result in a huge opportunity cost to you.

When looking at your calendar management efficiency, I want you to focus on billable hours. This is a very common term in the legal world, where lawyers bill the client only for the hours spent working for the client. Trust me, law firms are adamant that their young attorneys develop habits of spending most of their working hours on billable hours.

In the financial services industry, a financial advisor receives a billable hour for every kept appointment. Conversely, they earn only one billable hour for every 30 phone calls made to schedule appointments.

If you really want a wake-up call, I encourage you to review your last four weeks. For each week, punch in the hours from the time you reached the office or drove to your first appointment, until you arrived home at the end of the day. That number is your total hours worked. Then, give yourself one paid hour for each kept appointment and one hour for every 30 phone calls made.

You should be very aware of your billable hours going forward. For almost all reps, this is a demoralizing exercise. Think about it this way. If you find you work a 60-hour week but can give yourself credit for only 20 billable hours, that means you were paid for only 33% of the time away from your loved ones. You don't earn a dollar for the other two-thirds of the time you spent inefficiently.

When you develop that sense of awareness, you make better decisions. Study after study has been conducted on top producers to determine their daily efficiency and effectiveness. I want you to shoot for spending *at least* 60% on your billable hours. You can't get there overnight, but it's a great target to shoot for. You should sit back, strategize, and sincerely pay attention to this issue. As with every step

I teach in my system, I urge you to start by tracking it. If you can bring something to a heightened sense of awareness, you will always move the ball down the field in the right direction. If you're not privy to the critical levers in your business, you will continue receiving the same results. This billable hour concept is something I found very effective in coaching my advisors over the last two and a half decades.

The first step in the calendar management process is to create your ideal calendar. You always want to run toward something. You always want to have a goal set out that is very clearly identified as a perfect, most efficient scenario. That becomes your ideal calendar.

YOUR IDEAL CALENDAR

IN OFFICE	DOWNTOWN	IN OFFICE	DOWNTOWN	CERTAIN SUBURB	
Monday	Tuesday	Wednesday	Thursday	Friday	
xx	xx	x	x	x	7:00
	PHONING				10:30
	xx	xx	x	x	11:30
xx	xx	x	x		1:00
xx	x	x			2:20
xx		x			4:00
x	x	x			7:00
11	8	6	3	2	=30

Your ideal calendar should address multiple issues. First, each day of the week should include whether you are in the office or the specific community you plan to visit. For example, in my city of Chicago, my ideal calendar may denote Monday, Tuesday, and Wednesday as appointments at my downtown Chicago office. Thursday might be the northern suburbs, and Friday, the western suburbs. As you can imagine, with all your clients in one location, you have the opportunity to see many more people in less time by reducing travel time in between meetings. Therefore, you ideally want to arrange your calendar *geographically*.

The second issue is your timeslots. Like the doctor's office, arrange your day in timeslots according to when you see clients, when you have staff meetings, and when you telephone for new appointments. If you lack the proper staff and do your own case preparation, make the time on your calendar for case preparation as well. Some of my best reps who mastered this concept also had time in their day for personal activities, such as working out or worship. These reps really had their ideal calendar down and worked on living it out. It's critically important when you have staff that they also know exactly what your ideal calendar is.

One critical mistake I find reps make is thinking this is a great concept, so they have wonderful intentions as they construct their ideal calendar. Then, they make multiple bad decisions right out of the gate, and their staff sees it and begins to believe it's not very important.

Let me give you some examples. If you have a set time for phoning, but a client wants to see you during that time and you make that sacrifice – this can become a slippery slope. Number one: you're telling yourself, incorrectly, that phoning is unimportant. Phoning is critically important. Number two: you're indicating to your staff that it's not important because they see you ignoring phoning time. That's a cardinal sin to avoid at all costs.

Another bad mistake is canceling a scheduled staff meeting to meet with a client. Canceling staff meetings for other obligations tells your staff loud and clear that they're not nearly as important to you as your clients.

Therefore, when you put together an ideal calendar, it's important to do the best you can to live it from the start. It won't happen on day one, but each successive week you need to improve at living your calendar.

Additionally, be aware of how many weekly appointments you need to keep for your business plan to come to order. You don't want to rely on hope to hit your goals. Make sure it's a given that you'll hit your goals. You can control this by setting yourself up to schedule and keep the number of meetings necessary in a very realistic setting.

For example, if you know that you need to keep 15 meetings every week to hit your goal and that you have a cancellation rate of 50%, you also know that you must have 30 appointment slots in your ideal calendar every week. That way, after 50% of those cancel, you can still keep the 15 meetings.

I find there are some tricks of the trade for maintaining an ideal calendar. Here's what I want to teach you. First, this business is a momentum business. In my practice, I always try to make Mondays and Tuesdays my busiest days. My goal is to never keep fewer than 15 appointments a week. If I attend 10 or more by the end of Tuesday, I feel great about my business, and my momentum.

I encourage you to plan the first couple days of every week to work the most hours and see the most people. The first benefit is positive momentum. The second benefit is having the time to reschedule any Monday or Tuesday appointments when clients cancel due to issues beyond their control. The ability to meet them later in the week heightens your probability of keeping them and creates a subliminal message of a greater sense of urgency. As a result, my ideal calendar is much busier at the beginning of the week. Wednesday may slow down a little, with Thursday and Friday being the slowest days.

For your ideal calendar to work, you must bring it to life. In other words, it's one thing to set up this calendar, but it's another to implement it. Almost all the reps I coach set up their calendars rather quickly and fairly well, but that's only about 10% or 15% of the job. The hardest part of the job is to live it.

Here's my advice as to how to live your calendar. First, always know exactly where you stand in filling your ideal calendar. For example, if it's a Wednesday, I want you to know your ideal calendar for the following week. Let's assume that you have 30 slots for appointments. At the end of every day the previous week, know how many of those 30 slots you still need to book. You should also know which slots are open. When you have that sense of awareness, you have intentionality and a greater sense of urgency to pick up the phone and make additional appointments. You will relentlessly pursue a totally booked week by the end of your current week.

My second recommendation is to create a standing meeting every morning with your staff. When I do this, I limit the agenda to three to five items, and I want the meeting to last no longer than five to seven minutes. Your ideal calendar should be a line item on your agenda in standing staff meetings. To see how that would play out in your standing meeting, consider this example.

First thing in the morning – let's say 7 AM – you get together with your assistant and look at the following week's calendar. You are both in tune with how many slots are full and how many more slots need to be filled, as well as where they are and who is responsible for each. In my practice, I find it more common for the financial advisor to contact prospective clients, while the staff contacts existing clients to set up annual reviews and similar meetings.

This leads me to another important piece of the puzzle. You should know how many prospective client appointments are your responsibility and how many are your staff's responsibility. Once you've built the calendar and you and your staff know where you stand in relation to the calendar each day, the battle is 95% won. You are on the road to success, and you will sooner, rather than later, get to that point.

My last tip is to build incentive for your staff to fill that calendar. In an ideal calendar with 30 appointment slots that smoothly works the way you planned, and the following week has an ideal calendar set, consider offering an incentive bonus to your assistant. Not only does your assistant want to help you fulfill your own mission and purpose, but he or she should be financially motivated as well. Having this incentive in place will maintain a heightened sense of awareness for them as well.

My final comment on the ideal calendar is to put your phoning time in each and every day. Treat your phone time as if it's just as effective as when you meet with your A+ clients. Trust me, over time a rep who phones in a highly disciplined, dedicated, and consistent manner will have a much higher probability of an ideal calendar from an abundance standpoint, as well as a much higher probability of overall success.

When explaining the ideal calendar concept, I love to use a hotel analogy. Imagine if you run a hotel, one of the most crucial elements to manage is filling up every night. Every empty room is a cost or a lost opportunity. Your ideal calendar should be viewed in the same way. Any empty appointment slot is a cost/lost opportunity.

The second half of this module concerns phoning, which is critical to understand. I have some simple tips and tools that I have found to be helpful and effective.

First, understand that the only purpose of phoning is to get an appointment. When you have that mentality, your average time talking on the phone decreases. Your conversations become succinct, clear, and compelling, which allows you to place significantly more calls per day. It also allows you to project a professional and energetic tone to your clients. I find too many reps spend as much as 15 to 20 or, God forbid, even 30 minutes talking to a prospect, trying to convince them to meet. Instead, be very clear with your language and understand that the purpose of the call is not to sell financial products, or yourself. Rather, the sole purpose of the call is to *get the appointment.*

Second, I want you to understand that the phone is the gateway to doing what you need to do. Surgeons do not go to medical school excited about the fact that they must spend 10 to 15 minutes scrubbing down before surgery, but they understand it's an important part of their job. That's how I want you to look at your business. Too many reps get freaked out over the phone or hate the phone. Trust me, it's never going away. It's your most effective tool to make appointments. Once you accept that it's a necessary part of your job, you can move forward.

The goal of Phoning is simple:

To get the appointment

It's the GATEWAY

to what you really love to do!

Additionally, I want you to believe that, if you never get in front of a client, nothing will happen. However, if you successfully get in front of a client, you can change their life. Adopting this mentality created intensity about my phoning strategies. I gained a sense of competitiveness about phoning, combined with a deep desire to do everything I possibly could to get an appointment.

I believe integrity is one of the most important values in my life. However, phoning is one of the only times I feel it's okay to stretch the truth. For example, if I call someone to ask for an appointment, I might say, "I know you're in the AT&T building. I'm going to be there next Tuesday. Would 10 o'clock or 12 o'clock be better for you?" Even if I haven't planned to be there next Tuesday, I never regret or apologize for that sort of fib because I have the utmost faith and confidence that, if I let this individual off without getting an appointment, I don't have the opportunity to change their life.

Conversely, if I meet them, I have the opportunity to bring them to financial security, and they will never forget me. This knowledge gave me an intensity around my phoning that significantly helped me.

I'll repeat often throughout this book: I never want you to improvise anything. The two most critically important words you will hear throughout this book are *intentionality* and *sustainability*. Intentionality comes into play in the phoning module, big time. You want to sit down and design your language to be authentic, effective, and from your heart. You might not get it right the first time, so, like other things in your business, constantly test and tweak your language until you perfect it.

Ideally, your phoning language should be identical every single time. It should be laser-focused on nothing other than getting the appointment. Practice it so you don't come across like a horrible telemarketer. When settling on the language to use, remember that tone, inflection, and volume are essential. Even though they can't see you, the smile on your face and your passion can jump through the phone and grab them. That's when your phoning language will truly come alive. But you can't think about passion, purpose, and inflection until you first create a language script you're excited about.

At this point in many of my training sessions, people often ask, "Jim, what's your language?" You can get a taste of my language, which has been the same for some time, on my website and in my videos. Watching my delivery is much more effective than reading it in a book. Even so, I'll share it with you.

If Mary Jones recommended me to Bill Smith, and Bill answers my phone call, I'll say, "Hey, Bill, it's John Doe from such and such a company. I'm calling on behalf of Mary Jones. Did she get a chance to give you a call and tell you that I'd be calling?"

He might say, "No, who are you again?"

If so, I'll reply, "Well, that's too bad. I'll have to give Mary a hard time. She promised she was going to do that for me. I know you're busy, but now that I have you on the phone, I'm a financial representative with such and such company.

I work with Mary Jones. Mary has no reason to assume that you're interested in my services today; however, she spoke extremely highly of you. She knows exactly what it is that I do, and she believes that a meeting between the two of us would be mutually beneficial. I know that you happen to be in such and such building. I'm going to be out your way next Tuesday. Would 10 o'clock or 2 o'clock be better for you?"

So, that's my basic language. I want to leverage the nominator, while avoiding discussing what I do, or how I do it, or what products I have. I want to simply ask for the appointment and bank on the fact that the nominator is a close friend of theirs, which might be enough to get the appointment.

Once you have language established, you want to know how to overcome objections. Have your responses memorized backward, forward, sideways, and upside down. Let's face it; there are only a few types of objections you'll get throughout your career. You'll encounter thousands of objections, but most of them will be ones you've heard before, and they should never throw you for a loop.

Let's go through those briefly here. Once again, without seeing and listening to my delivery, these may be difficult to envision, but the descriptions will arm you with the ammo necessary to fend off these common objections. Just put your own personal spin on them.

Objection one: "I'm all set. I have no need for financial services."

Simply respond, "Listen, Mary had no reason to assume you had a need whatsoever, nor did I. But things have a way of changing over time. She thought that it was a great use of our time to get together today. Having said that, I know you're in such and such building. If Tuesday doesn't work, is Wednesday at 1 o'clock or 3 o'clock better for you?"

By saying this and attempting to set up another appointment, I'm simply establishing that it doesn't matter if the client has a need or not. I assure them that Mary the nominator didn't indicate a need either. I make sure they know I'm not calling to sell them something, but to meet because I've heard great things about them. This phone call will be the seed of a future relationship, whether they have a need now or in five or seven years.

Objection two: "I already have an advisor I'm happy with."

I would simply say, "You know what, Mr. Prospect? I would be shocked if you didn't. Mary spoke extremely highly of you as a top-caliber individual. I expected you to already have a rep, but here's what I found over my career with people who already have an advisor. After they meet with me, one of two things happen: either they get the recognition and validation that the individual they're working with is doing a great job and they feel that much better about it or I identify some needs that perhaps their existing financial advisor hasn't recognized. The way I look at it, Mr. Prospect, neither is a bad outcome.

"Therefore, if Tuesday at 1 o'clock or 3 o'clock doesn't work for you, would Wednesday at 2 o'clock or 4 o'clock be better?" This is an example of how I react to that particular objection.

I want you to have a little intestinal fortitude. You should be able to go all the way to three objections with every client you call. People are programmed to say "no" the first time, and most people object the second time, but they often come through on your third swing. Successful people appreciate somebody who has passion and will relentlessly pursue what they want. Believe it or not, it's more of a turn-on than a turn-off as long as you maintain a professional approach.

What about their third objection?

I cannot tell you how many of my best clients I landed after hearing a third objection.

When they give me a third objection, I simply say, "Mr. or Mrs. Prospect, things have a way of changing over time. Would you have any objection if I kept in touch with you every six months?"

Nearly 98% of the time, they say, "No problem." Put them back in your system and call them every six months.

I've had lots of fun with people I would literally call for four or five years before they would grant me a meeting. The phone calls simply sound like the ones described above. We laugh together, and six months later the process repeats. I finally just break them down.

You must carefully choose whom to pursue this way. You don't want to pursue a client of average caliber or, God forbid, lower than average. But for your best referrals, it requires some creativity. That's only one example of applying creativity to put you into a spot to get that appointment. In terms of phoning, simply make calls at the same time, every time. I suggest paring your script down and improving to the point where you can consistently recite it with real passion and purpose. Understand exactly what to say to client objections, and *always reach the third objection* if necessary.

When you hear the third objection and still don't have the appointment, ask if you can keep in touch. Put them back in your system for six months and follow through. By doing so, you will program people with whom you follow through and do what you say, which is another attractive element.

I believe it's also important for you to assess your ratios.

Look at your business occasionally and check your effectiveness. With today's technology and caller ID, you'll reach referrals on new prospective client calls only 20% of the time. It's not because they're not there when you call; rather, it's because they don't recognize your number. They're not waiting for your call, and you did not get the right nomination. Therefore, they don't answer. It could be instead that you called the wrong number. Perhaps you have a work line instead of a cell phone, or you have a cell phone instead of a work line. The bottom line is that you need to ensure the nominator provides the correct phone number to call your referrals.

On average, you should make appointments with new

prospective clients 50% of the time when you reach them. Using these numbers, if you make 30 phone calls in an hour to give yourself a billable hour, you would most likely have six conversations. That's 20% of the 30 calls. You should end up with three appointments from those six, which would be 50%. Know and track those numbers, because that determines whether your efforts are working.

I want to leave you two tricks of my trade: one is leaving messages and two is confirming appointments.

A lot of reps ask me, "Hey, how often should I leave messages?"

That's somewhat of a gray area. You certainly don't want to leave more than one message per day, because it may look as if you're stalking them. You probably don't want to leave a message more than once every three business days, but you'll have to play with that and see what works best for you.

When you do leave a message, here is what I find works the best. If Mary Jones referred me to Bill Smith, and I needed to leave him a message, I would say, "Hey, Bill, it's Jim Effner, financial advisor with such and such company. I'm calling on behalf of the nomination I received from Mary Jones. I believe she's already reached out to you and told you I'd be calling but do me a favor if she hasn't. Please pick up the phone and give her a call first. She'll bring you up to speed with what this is all about, and then go ahead and call me. Here's my number. I can't wait to hear from you."

That tends to force a conversation between the referral and the nominator, and I find that works well. When confirming an appointment, you should assume consent. The only reason you're calling is to clarify the address. Thus, if I'm calling Bill Smith to confirm an appointment tomorrow in my office at 2 o'clock, I don't call him and say, "Hey, Bill, it's Jim. I just want to make sure we're still on. Are we still good?" This approach gives them an out.

Instead, I leave this message, "Hey, Bill, I'm super excited about our meeting. I can't wait to meet you. I have heard such great things about you. Our meeting is at 2 o'clock, but I couldn't remember if I gave you my address, so I simply want to get back to you. Again, here it is. See you tomorrow!" That is a much more effective way to confirm appointments, as opposed to asking them if you're still meeting.

One more thing: remember that the main purpose of mastering your phoning language is about you, not the perspective client. I have found that a rep who masters their phoning language gains a tremendous level of confidence when they phone. If you know exactly what you're going to say and are totally prepared to handle any objection that comes your way, you eliminate most of your fears. I realize this might seem to some like a remedial skill (though success always comes back to being strong in the basics), but trust me, it's critically important. Consider this: PGA tour players spend 1,000 hours per year practicing three-foot putts because they are so important. View your phoning as a three-foot putt.

So, there you have the complete second module. At the

end of this chapter, I put together a one-page system for phoning and calendar management. I encourage you to set it aside and refer to it when you find you're not being efficient with your calendar or opportunities arise to improve in your phoning. Good luck on that!

SYSTEM FOR PHONING AND CALENDAR MANAGEMENT

1. Create your ideal calendar.
2. Have a relentless desire to fill appointment slots for the following week.
3. Do not compromise your planned time slots and locations to meet the needs of clients.
4. Schedule your phoning time and honor it as if it were an A+ client.
5. Use identical phoning language every time and always end with two time slots that need to be filled.
6. Memorize your response to the top three to five objections. Use them consistently.
7. Always go through three objections.
8. If necessary, stand up while phoning. The volume, tone, inflections, and passion you exude on the phone is important.

BRIDGE YOUR GAP • JIM EFFNER

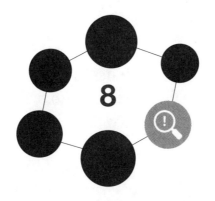

8

FACT-FINDING

I have had a number of people ask me whether I missed being out in the field after I went full-time into leadership. My answer is always the same: I love being in leadership, but the one thing I miss most is executing the fact-finder interview with a new prospective client. Sometimes in the industry this is called a *data-gathering* meeting or an *information-gathering* meeting. I happen to refer to it as a *fact-finder* meeting, but they all mean the same thing.

I truly believe that being able to connect with a client over a fact-finder meeting is a gift, although it comes with the highest level of responsibility. The gift is the fact that we really get to see an intimate relationship being formed. We get to ask clients questions that even their best friends and other family members don't get to ask them. We get to learn about the inner person. I really enjoy this stage of the business. It truly is my favorite part of all six stages of the sales cycle.

We will break the fact-finder module into multiple sections, but conceptually we're going to begin with what I'm going to call the *approach*. Before I go into that, I want to tell you that the most important thing advisors can do during the fact-finder is *leave their needs at the door*. Far too often I see financial advisors using the fact-finder meeting as an excuse to manipulate the client. So many times, reps focus on what they need to say and the questions they need to ask to land the client. They try to convince their lead that he or she needs whatever the rep most wants to sell. This could not be a worse mistake.

This misguided and dangerous technique is one of the single largest reasons our industry gets a bad reputation. With this in mind, before you walk into the fact-finder meeting with a new client, you must leave *your* needs outside that door and remain totally focused on the client's needs.

To truly focus on the client's needs, we must work on developing our skill sets around being completely present in the meeting. Don't let your mind wander to earlier events, tasks you still need to get done before going to your next meeting, or whatever is going on in your personal life. You need to give this person the gift of your presence. It's one of the most precious gifts you can give anyone, as it makes him or her feel as if they were the only person that exists on the planet during the hour that you were with them. Truly listen by truly trying to understand everything they say. This is the mindset we want when we go in. The reason being, other than the fact that it is the right thing to do, that you then don't need to create an artificial need for your help. You will have listened and truly understood their pain points and be able to better help your lead understand that they really need your help.

Almost 100% of the clients in the more than 3,000 fact-finder interviews I did in the first decade of my career had financial problems and needs. This is consistent with everybody in our country. Understanding this is important so we don't have to manipulate people into working with a financial planner. All you need is to be genuine and listen to your client. They will tell you what they need.

Before we discuss the fact-finder interview, the first thing I want to talk about is the approach. I want you to be able to use specific, powerful language to describe to the client what you do, how you do it, and why you do it. Your words should be concise and compelling.

The purpose of the approach is to be able to change the client's mindset from negative to positive. Perhaps 100% of new prospective clients are not skeptical, but you will be better served if you just assume everyone is.

Most of your prospective clients will have the following mindset:

"Why did I agree to do this?"

"How quick can I get out of this?"

"This person is just going to try to sell me something."

And the worst of all, "This person is not honest."

So now you need to switch them to a positive mindset that will have them sitting on the edge of their chair thinking:

"Where has this person been all my life?"

"I wish I would have met them a long time ago."

"This is exactly what I need."

"This is the type of person that I could see myself working with for a long time."

We do this partly through the words that we say, but we do it even more by how we make them feel. Just like everything I teach, you cannot approach this as if you are merely an actor. You must be genuine. You must have clear inflections in your voice and tone, reinforced by your body language, posture, and the smile on your face. The eye-contact you make with your prospective client reflects the amount of passion, purpose, and genuineness in the deepest part of your heart.

Before each fact-finder interview, I want you to think about the letters D.N.A., and I'm not talking about the scientific version of DNA. I'm talking about Different, New, and Attractive. Your goal is to make your approach full of D.N.A. (A close friend, Dr. Bob Chiron, developed this concept and has been kind enough to let me use it in my teachings throughout the years – thanks, Bob!)

Let's start with the D – Different. It is said that people are naturally attracted to the new and the different in peo-

Your **approach** must describe:

- What you do
- How you do it
- The benefit of working with you
  (with tools to illustrate it)

In a way that is

DIFFERENT
NEW
ATTRACTIVE

ple and in the world around them. Below is a transcript of how I recommend you go about setting yourself apart. After I have explained to my prospect exactly what I do, I continue with this monologue:

"I really appreciate your time today. Mrs. [use the name of the referral nominator] spoke very highly of you. I know you are incredibly busy and I appreciate you taking the time to meet with me. The way I do business is that the first time I get together with someone, I simply ask a lot of questions and I try to do a very effective job of listening. What's important to me in the meeting today is that I walk away and feel that I completely understand where you're at and where you want to go. I want to understand the feelings you have about where you have been and where you want to go. Once I understand you, I feel I can combine the logical side of financial planning with the emotional side. All this information will be confidential, of course, and when I leave, one of three things will happen. We might agree that there's a sense of urgency to get back together and in a short period of time, so we will do so. The second scenario might be that we agree that there is a need, but the timing is not appropriate and we will table it for a later date. And third, perhaps either you or I will feel it's not a potential fit and I will chalk it up as just another contact in a relationship, and we will go our own ways.

"But if and when we get back together the next time, I will have put together a plan for you. What my clients love about that plan is I get them to step out of the busy merry-go-round of their life and go up to 30,000 feet, allowing them to look down on their financial life. You will see where you really are and what you need to change in order to meet your goals. What my clients love about that process is that I'm able to make it comprehensive, yet simple to understand. Almost all my clients feel this is the first time they've had that type of experience. After that meeting, we will determine whether these issues match your personal priorities, and then we'll get together a third time for an implementation stage, taking action, moving, and solving those issues.

"The last step of my process is getting together with my clients each and every year in an 'annual review.' What is unique about my process is that I've created a financial security-planning checklist outlining the ultimate plan to be financially secure. Every year in our annual review, we will review our progress. I also hope my clients understand that financial security is a journey that may take 30, 35, even 40 years to achieve. My clients love seeing their progress, and I keep in tune with their lives, including personal, professional, and financial changes along the way.

"In addition to continuing to build our relationship, that's the process I use, Mr. Prospect."

That's a long way to communicate my approach, but I can't tell you how important it is. You never get a second chance to make a first impression. You need to do this well, and you need to deliver it with purpose and passion. I strongly urge you to practice it.

Know Your Goal

The most important concept of mastering the fact-finder meeting, and I share this many times in my training, is to begin with the end in mind. Your goal should be: if you can walk away from your fact-finder meeting and have the prospective client say these three things about you, you are 99% certain of retaining them as a client.

1) That person totally understands me!

2) That person genuinely cared about me!

3) That person was very knowledgeable about his or her profession!

When you get a possible client to say those three things after you leave, you are almost all the way there to adding a new client to your practice.

Fact-finder Process

Now that I've outlined your approach and your goals, let's dig into the first part of the actual fact-finder meeting.

The Introduction

The introduction is the opportunity to get to know the prospects better – financially and in many ways personally – than perhaps anyone has known them. This should happen prior to going into any types of numbers, finances, or benefits they will receive from your services. (Keep in mind that you don't ever want to start selling anything during the fact-finder meeting!) You want to start by getting to know them. This comes down to asking questions in categories such as family, career, future plans (call this their "vision"), and hobbies. Ask what they like to do for fun.

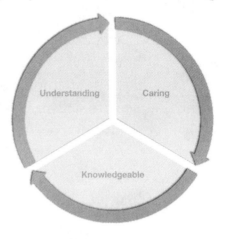

In every stage of the fact-finder your job is to instill these 3 feelings:
Understanding, Caring, Knowledgeable

There are many different types of questions you can ask prospects in this particular section, but I feel that the bigger interpersonal risks you take, the deeper you can go, and the more you can get them to reveal to you, the better planner you can become for them. The more they feel that you understand and care about them, the more likely they will be to sign on with you. Remember D.N.A.? People buy what is different. Very few financial reps actually do this, and implementing it will set you apart.

I'll leave you with a few ideas for each of these categories.

Family

In the family category, there is, of course, the obvious: "Tell me about your spouse, your children, your mother and father." Get their children's names and dates of birth. These are typical questions and are good to ask.

However, after you ask the family questions, one of my favorite questions is: "Mr. Prospect, obviously I'm in the business of financial planning, so one of the questions I'd like to start with is, 'Could you tell me a little bit about – even from your first memory – what you learned about money from your parents?'"

Then shut up. Sit back and listen.

After your prospect has talked for a while, you can ask them questions like, "What do you want to continue doing that you learned from them?" and "What did you learn from them that you absolutely don't want to repeat?"

Other helpful questions you can ask are "Tell me, Mr. Prospect, what differences do you and your spouse have when it comes to finances? Has this had an impact on your planning?" and "How can a financial advisor like me help with that?" Or you can ask, "If there are no differences, how did you two get connected on your financial planning philosophies?"

These questions provide you with valuable information and are also questions that nobody has asked them.

Career

The obvious questions are about what they do for a living. However, many young reps I mentored would come back and tell me that their potential client was an attorney, without knowing what type of law they practiced. They missed out on knowing if their client was a non-profit lawyer, divorce attorney, or a litigator! I used to teach my mentees to find out details they cannot find on the internet. For example, when asking about a potential client's career, pose questions such as "What specific area of law do you litigate?" and "How did you become interested in that? Did you go to school to get into that area specifically or did it just happen?"

Ask about their favorite and least favorite part of the job. These are the types of questions that will get you to know your potential client. People love to talk about themselves and very rarely does someone genuinely listen and ask interesting questions like these.

Future Plans and Vision

Simply ask your prospect to describe their career dreams and goals. What do they see themselves doing 5, 10, and 15 years down the road? Ask questions such as "What do you think might get in the way?" "What excites you about this and what scares you about it?" and "Is there anything

I can do to help?"

As a successful financial planner, you should have connections in your community. Perhaps you know people in fields that the prospect is interested in and you might be able to help the prospect get together with your contacts at some point.

Hobbies

"What do you like to do for fun?" while simple, is actually a great question to ask, because, once again, it helps you to get to know the prospect on a personal level. But you also get to build some *similarities*. Keep this point in mind as you ask about their hobbies. For example, if you are both very interested in golf, you probably know some of the same courses and have probably played at some of the same golf clubs. You might even know some of the members at a golf club and can build some connections that way as well.

Past Experiences with a Financial Advisor

Before getting into the heart of the fact-finder meeting, I like to ask clients about their past experience with financial advisors. Reps should understand what the prospect expects of them.

But if you're going to ask that question, you must learn how to ask in a way that elicits a genuine and illuminating response, because often all the answers will be similar. "I expected them to be honest." "I wanted to trust them." "I didn't want them to try to always sell me stuff."

When the prospect gives these predictable answers, I think it's good to say things like "It's interesting that you said that." "Why did you pick that?" "What does that really mean to you?" "Tell me how that would play out." "Have you had experiences similar to that in the past?"

These are questions – probing for the reasons behind their stock answers – that will help you understand what you must do to work with them.

After learning more about what is expected of you and how you may outperform your competition, you will go into the next stage of our fact-finder meeting, which is asking about education goals. But before I go there, I want to emphasize that the purpose of the fact-finder interview is simply to figure out where they are today – not only emotionally, but logically – in areas such as their net worth in assets and benefits, then drill down for details. Without this information, we won't be able to help them understand their long-term goals.

I believe there are four or five categories you should consistently talk about when your clients are married with children, including:

1.) college education planning for children

2.) retirement planning

3.) survivor income planning

4.) disability income planning

5.) long-term care planning for clients north of the age of 50

Let's start with education. The first thing we want to do is make sure our clients are realistic about their goals. I have found that many clients are unrealistic, especially if they do not have children yet or have very young children. They typically have no idea what college really costs.

Therefore, we have to make sure their goals are realistic. If a young couple has an eight-year-old and they haven't planned for college, you cannot skip over this issue if they tell you they want to fully fund their child's education at a private college. You need to help them understand what that will take and how unrealistic that probably is.

We also want to determine where each particular client lies on what I call the "wishful-thinking scale" – with zero being very wishful thinking, such as "it would be nice, but I don't have a prayer," and 10 being "I will run through a brick wall if necessary to get it done."

When my clients describe their goals, I want to know where they land on this scale so I can truly help with what is actually important to them. So, I ask some preliminary questions even before asking about their goals.

I ask questions such as, "Where did you go to school?" or "How much does that school cost today?" "How was your school paid for?" "How do you feel about that today?" I also think you can ask clients: "If you're not able to fully fund your child's education, what is your strategy to fund, or help fund, the Gap?"

I trained my reps to understand that only 1 to 3% of

their clients were going to be able to fully fund their children's college education from savings. However, 90% of their clients' children were still going to go to college. Therefore, acknowledging the Gap between their savings and the cost of education is something almost every one of your clients will have to do. As their financial advisor, urging your clients to talk about this is your job. So, when asking them about their education goals, you are simply asking them what they want to do.

Remember, when you partake in these fact-finders, it's vital to leave your needs at the door! It's also very important to be nonjudgmental and absolutely not place your values on theirs. Simply listen and make sure the prospect's answers are very real from their perspective.

Imagine your prospect tells you that they fully funded their own college education. You should then realize they probably expect their kids to pay for college as well. This is their prerogative, so as a professional, that's simply what you write down. It is not your job to convince them to do otherwise.

But if they say they'd like to pay for all, or a portion, or perhaps just pay for room and board, your questions should form around this information. For instance, "How many years do you have to save money?" or "What about graduate school?" "Private college or public university?"

Simply ask the questions to clearly understand their goals. This is your job.

The next section we're going into is retirement. Obviously, this is a major area of conversation with any client. First, we want to know what the *prospect thinks about retirement*. We want to have an honest dialogue. This includes prompting them to give us as meaningful an answer as possible, even if they haven't thought about retirement yet.

What I enjoy most about discussing retirement with my clients is that everybody has a story. Depending on a client's age, it could be about their grandma and grandpa, or mom and dad, or even in-laws. Your clients have a perspective on planning appropriately for retirement from older family members. They probably also have an idea of what it's like to be inappropriately prepared, as well as the consequences of not preparing for retirement. Motivate your clients to discuss retirement by asking them about their parents' situation. Ask them how financially comfortable they are. If they're not comfortable, ask why they think that is. What did they learn from their parents?

If they are very young, ask about grandparents and in-laws. Urging your clients to tell the stories about how they've been impacted by witnessing older family members will help you understand them better and will also give them the gift of starting to think about the importance of retirement planning.

Let's face it, to be financially successful in retirement you must learn how to make self-sacrifices and embrace delayed gratification. Most Americans have no clue what that's like. Your client's ability to touch those emotional purse strings through this process will be the greatest impact you can have on their lives. (This, by the way, is why I believe there is no future for computer-based financial planning. No computer will ever be able to do what you can do properly in this fact-finder meeting if you have the right approach.)

Once we have Mr. or Mrs. Prospect talking about and seriously thinking about retirement, we want to learn about their specific goals. These goals simply include the following:

1) What age would you like to be able to retire?
2) What income would you like to have at retirement?
3) How long do you want to be able to plan for retirement?

Be prepared for surprising answers to these questions. Sometimes clients will tell you they never want to retire, while sometimes clients will give you a very unrealistic age. For example, they may want to retire at 45 or 50 but have no family money and they're not good savers! It's important that you address both of these issues. For individuals who say they never want to retire, I recommend you explain to them that the definition of retirement is working every single day because you want to go to work, not because you have to. As a financial advisor, you value having options. Therefore, you will help them plan so that at a certain age they are working only because they love their work. For individuals with an unrealistic early age for retirement, your goal is to help them understand exactly what it will take, and whether it is even possible.

Often times, I meet with clients in their early 30s who say they want to retire at 50 but have no assets set aside. They would literally have to save more than what their current income is in order to accomplish that. So, I explain these numbers to them and they soon get the drift. They want to start planning but they never thought about it and they look to you as the expert.

What I recommend that you say to these clients is "Listen, we don't know where life will lead us, but a general rule we can use is that you will retire at age 65. Let's use 75% of your income today adjusted, for inflation, and project that amount out 20 years, to age 85, to arrive at a figure. You will have to believe in a retirement plan. You don't necessarily have to use my plan, but the one I just shared with you works for me."

Now we want to collect information about the prospective clients' assets and liabilities in order to get a better picture of where they are financially. I would really like you to use these two words at this point: snapshot and movie. I used to play a game with the reps I mentored and coached when they came into the office after a fact-finder interview with a balance sheet listing assets and liabilities. I would ask them these questions.

For example, let's say a rep interviews a prospect with $50,000 in their savings account. I ask the rep how the prospect amassed $50,000. If the rep says, "I don't know, I just wrote down the number," that rep is just being an uncaring robot. If you really want to show the client that you care about and understand them, ask them three or four questions about every figure they give you.

Learn why, for example, client A and client B both have $50,000 in their savings accounts at the age of 30.

Perhaps client A became frustrated years before for overspending and committed to a budget, which included saving $1,000 per month.

Client B has $50,000 in a savings account, and his grandfather died nine months ago, leaving him a $250,000 inheritance – but he's already blown $200,000. As you can imagine, these are two dramatically different types of people, despite their similar snapshots in time.

Ask questions such as how the client reached that number and how it would be broken down. In terms of liabilities, you can ask questions about exactly when debt needs to be paid back and at what rate. You can ask many different questions about numbers, but make sure that you do everything possible to understand them.

Now we move on to understanding prospective clients' income. Their income really is a status symbol, often not reflecting their true financial state. For example, if somebody makes $100,000, that means nothing to them or to you, at least not in the long run. The most important number you need to know is their monthly net cash flow after 401(k), taxes, health insurance, and other deductions. This represents the amount coming into the household and deposited into their checking account. This is the most crucial number for you to understand.

This is very important. Once you know how much cash comes into the household and have a clear assessment of their assets and liabilities, you will know how much of that money they're spending. You'll know that the money in their 401(k) and equity in their house on the balance sheet does not come out of their monthly cash flow *if it's taken out before they get it.* And if there are no other assets and existing credit card debt, you know that they spend more than they're bringing home. If they have substantial money in a savings account, perhaps a brokerage account and other investments, and you know the story behind them, you'll know how much they're saving in discretionary cash flow on a monthly basis.

This is the most critical component reps miss out on. There is an art to it, yet it's not that difficult; you simply stay committed to people who are straight salary. If they receive salaries and bonuses, you need to figure out when they get the bonuses, along with the history of the bonuses. The most likely future of the bonuses they may receive can be tougher to understand. You see, you have to apply the theory that past behavior is the most indicative of future results and try to ask a lot of questions around that theory.

But it's also critically important to look for any changes that might come in the future. In other words, you may have a married couple and one of them will stay home when they have their first child.

Later in the meeting, ask them about survivor income – life insurance. It's a huge mistake to impose your views on them at this time. All you simply want to do is ask them question after question to get to the truth about their needs.

So, let's assume you know their needs and are able to have a very meaningful conversation as we go into the survivor income section. First, find out what insurance benefits they have through their employer and what they have individually purchased. This is another area where the questions and follow-up questions become very important, because it's about urging them to tell you why they bought what they bought, the experience of buying insurance, what they struggled with in buying it, what they do not want to duplicate the next time, and so on.

It truly centers on understanding what they have.

Here's another useful question when meeting with young clients without life insurance: Ask them why they have not done anything, not in a negative tone, but to sincerely understand what has been difficult for them about buying insurance. In this way, you can really get to know them.

The most effective way to ask how they would take care of their spouse if they don't make it home tonight is to hold up a mirror showing their current household finances and put it this way: "Mr. Prospect, out of the current $5,000 monthly net cash flow you live on now, how much of that would you want to continue for your spouse if you do not make it home tonight?"

Then simply wait for the response. The only two things we need to find out in this category are how much of that they want and for how long. Some will tell you immediately, "All of it," and some will have a different answer.

What's important is that you draw out the truth from their hearts and roll with it. This will be a fun experience for you, as well as an eye-opening experience for your clients. More often than not, they've never been asked that question and never even thought about it. Some clients will give you a response like, "I have no idea. You're the expert, you tell me what it should be."

There are three areas when evaluating the need for a death benefit, debt reduction, educational cost, and income replacement. I would say that a good benchmark is about 80% of their current budget, which assumes that the individual who theoretically passes away would consume about 20% of that budget. Let's face it; with two adults in the household, little kids, and two cars, they won't need two cars if there's only one spouse.

So I simply say, "Mr. Prospect, either we project that out until the youngest child is out of the house, defined by age 21, or we project that out until your spouse reaches age 65, or we project it out for the remainder of your spouse's life expectancy. It's up to you to decide which is most important."

Clients will get defensive if they see they are nowhere close to financial stability and they know they still don't want to buy life insurance, so they may flippantly respond, "My spouse is super educated. She'll be fine." When you get a response like this, you just need to do your job, which is to not judge and make sure that what they are telling you is the truth.

This can be a sticky situation. You can ask the spouses if they have had this discussion. Some people may say, "My spouse's parents are loaded, so they will take care of her." You can have conversations about this by asking if they have that in writing – but you do need to be able to pull that out of them to determine if they're saying that to get you to stop talking life insurance, or if it's the truth.

This is where I feel the rubber hits the road on the true definition of a loving household full of family values. When you have that situation, you are armed with what you need to put some accurate information into their plan.

The next area is the disability income section. What we need to do here is start out with what they have. This is a great opportunity to deliver what I mentioned earlier from the three categories where you have become knowledgeable about the clients' circumstances.

Much of the time, people have not purchased an individual disability plan. They know they have something through work, but they know nothing about it. This is an area of opportunity to tell them a little bit about how typical group disability insurance works. Explain the differences between short-term and long-term, the standard percentages in each category, the pros and cons about an employer plan, and when it's taxable and not taxable. You're probably providing them with an abundance of new information, which will help them feel that you're knowledgeable about what you do. Getting them to understand the products they currently have (if they even know!) will make this section relatively simple for you.

If they don't know exactly what disability plan they have, try to make a few assumptions that can be further substantiated once you have all the facts through a brief conversation. For example, if they tell you they have short- and long-term disability, but they don't know the exact percentages, you might assume that the short-term is at 100% and the long-term is 60%, because those are standard plans. Then you can simply say this in the meeting.

I use a scratch pad and draw three arrows on it. The very far left arrow represents what they bring home per month. Using the previous example of $5,000 per month, I would say, "Mr. Prospect, this is what you're currently bringing home at $5,000. Based on my brief analysis so far, it takes your household that entire amount of money to run. Based on the event of a disability lasting beyond six months, your group policy gives you 60%, which is $3,000 per month, but because you don't pay the premiums, it's taxable, so net after-tax you would have about $2,500."

The left arrow would have $5,000 on it, the middle arrow $2,500, and the third arrow would be the Gap, which is an additional $2,500. Then I would simply say, "Mr. Prospect, I don't know about you, but based on what I've learned so far, God forbid a disability were to occur, it seems as if it would be an issue in your household financially. Does that concern you?"

More often than not the client will reply, "Yeah, that would be a concern." Sometimes they'll say, "It's kind of a concern, but it depends on how much it costs." Or they might say, "It's not really a concern, I don't ever see becoming disabled."

It's at that point that you don't want to go into the mode of selling them disability, but you do want to have a conversation that goes something like this:

"You know what, Mr. Prospect, I understand how you feel and I quite frankly feel the same way. I have a white-collar job, and I think that if I was disabled I could sit at a desk and still do my job. However, I don't know if you know anybody who's had cancer and chemotherapy, or even if you can go back to the last time you had a 103° temperature and just didn't feel like going in to work. If we can put together a financial plan that makes you bulletproof if something like that happens, you can focus on your health and not have to worry about money. It just makes sense to me to at least look at what that would take, wouldn't you agree?"

And almost 100% of the time, my clients will respond, "Yeah, let's take a look at that." The reason why, of course, is that it just makes sense.

So now we have reached the end of the hypothetical fact-finder meeting. You may call this whatever you want: a wrap-up, summary, or executive summary. I like to call it the discovery agreement. This is a critically important part of the fact-finder, because if you think about it, you have spent more than an hour with somebody you've met for the first time. You gathered information that they haven't shared with anybody else. You asked them some deep, personal questions covering a broad array of categories, and if you just leave, a couple problems may surface. Number one, you don't really know what to come back for; number two, they're confused about everything that transpired;

and number three, they might not necessarily have an appropriate sense of urgency, leading to continued procrastination in setting up the next meeting.

The purpose of the discovery agreement is – in a very concise, compelling, and clear fashion – to create an executive summary about our meeting that intensifies a sense of urgency and clarity to the client's expectations for the next meeting. Therefore, I will share in my own words.

Once again, this is an important area that I demonstrate more effectively via video on my website – so check it out!

I would say to Mr. Prospect, "We spent an hour and a half together today and we discussed a great deal. Before I leave, let me sum up what I learned, to make sure you and I are on the same page now and when we get together next time.

"It's going to be very relevant. The first category we covered was the goals you and your spouse have for the education of your three children. You told me that it was important to educate them to the extent of 50% of the total cost, and you want to do that for four years for each kid. You told me the story about how your parents did that for you and feel that's what you want to do for your kids. Am I correct?

"The second item we talked about is retirement. You have thought a lot about retirement, but you understand that starting to plan for it now is important. We used a benchmark of 65 years old, at 80% of your current income, and you gave me the balances of your current 401(k) and

IRA, so we'll be taking a look at those.

"The third category we talked about, Mr. Prospect, was what if, God forbid, you don't make it home tonight? What would you want to happen in your household for your family to be okay? You mentioned that you wanted to have $4,000 a month until your spouse is 65 years old, and you said that you still wanted to educate the three kids at 50%. You told me about the insurance you have at work and about the individual policy you bought from your multi-line agent where you also have your homeowner's insurance. Am I correct? Great.

"Last but not least, we talked about the disability section. You mentioned knowing you had it through work, but you didn't think you had anything else. I talked to you about the Gap that would occur in the event of a disability; so therefore, we need to work on making sure we can cover that Gap. Is that correct, Mr. Prospect?

"What we will do in the next meeting is take all that information and I will put it in a very thorough plan that will allow you to jump up to 30,000 feet and look at your family's financial life to give you a very clear understanding of what we need to do in order for you to get an A in each one of those categories. My clients love seeing this plan and I'm excited about showing it to you.

"Before I leave, is there anything I missed in that wrap-up or are we on the same page?"

You never want to leave a loop open where either you or your staff needs to get back in touch with the prospect later. You want to ink a date on the calendar, a location, and a time before you leave. This is where many of the reps I trained claimed that the client wanted the next meeting to be with their spouse, yet they don't know their spouse's calendar. In this instance, I suggest encouraging the client to make an educated guess. Most spouses know each other's schedule and can make an educated guess. The worst-case scenario would be rescheduling a meeting in order to deliver the plan. Additionally, you should also have a yellow pad to highlight all the areas of information they need to provide that they didn't have in the fact-finder meeting.

SYSTEM FOR FACT-FINDING

1. Leave your needs at the door. Fully dedicate the meeting to your client's needs.
2. Begin with consistent approach language that explains what you do, how you do it, and the benefit of working with you.
3. Create an experience that leaves them feeling that you understand them, care about them and are knowledgeable.
4. Ask follow-up questions in order to truly understand your client's story.
5. Use questions to uncover the gap between where your clients are and where they want to be in the areas of survivor income, college education, and retirement.
6. Help your clients understand their financial gap in the event of a long-term disability.
7. Have a follow-up process to compile all outstanding information that you were unable to obtain in the meeting.
8. Communicate your discovery agreement in a way that summarizes the meeting and sets the expectation for the next steps.
9. If the fact-finding opened one or more cases, schedule the following meeting prior to departing.

BRIDGE YOUR GAP • JIM EFFNER

BRIDGE YOUR GAP • JIM EFFNER

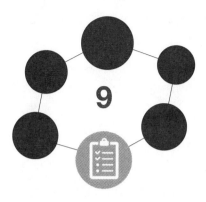

PLANNING

As we look at the planning module, we should begin with the assumption that a planning meeting will occur within a week after completing the initial data-gathering fact-finder meeting.

We want to bring a sense of clarity to our last discussion. I often start by telling the client, "I'm not naïve enough to think that all you've thought about is our last conversation," before asking if I can begin the current meeting with a brief summary.

I often refer to the summary as the introduction to the plan. The first purpose of summarizing is to review and clarify everything discussed in the previous meeting. The second goal is to prove to a prospect or client that we listened effectively during the first meeting.

In other words, we should demonstrate that we have successfully captured all the factual and emotional information expressed to us in the planning meeting. Once we've provided the summary, the client should feel we have a better understanding of them and that we truly listened.

We also summarize in order to come across as true professionals. If we merely come back to them with a bundle of products based on what we *think* they need, they perceive us as nothing more than common salespeople. If we truly want to maximize this space, we must come across as true advisors.

That leads us into the final reason for the planning meeting: effective communication of the client's problems in relation to their financial goals. You receive the most value as a financial advisor when a client perceives you as an effective listener capable of understanding their situation. You must be able to show the client the strategic gaps in their situation and explain the changes necessary to achieve their financial goals. You become the client's advocate by helping them solve the problems for the reasons you've outlined previously.

In sum, the purpose of this plan is to bring clarity to the client with respect to their gaps and to guide them in owning those gaps so they will not feel as if they're being sold unnecessary products. I liken it to an MRI in the medical world. If a patient is having trouble with his knee, the MRI identifies and illuminates the problem and thereby creates in the patient the desire to fix the problem, along with the clarity to understand the options for doing so.

Let's begin with the way I prefer to deliver an introduction to my clients.

I like to use the following analogy.

"Mr. Prospect, as we go into this plan, one of the things you are going to learn is what it will take for you to get an 'A' in each section of the plan."

The reason I prefer this approach is that most clients can remember their school days and recall their desire to earn an "A" in every subject tested. I spend a brief time reminding them that not every student receives an "A" in every class, but successful, driven students at least start out with an effort to do so. Next, I explain that very few of my clients have an "A" in every aspect of their planning, but that I believe it's my job to help them understand, at least initially, what it takes to achieve an "A" grade.

The second goal of my introduction is to provide a consistent summary, encompassing every topic discussed in the fact-finder interview. But don't make the mistake of believing that you should bury the client in "facts."

Where I believe most reps make a huge mistake during the summary segment is taking an *overly logical approach* during a process that involves very little logic on the part of the client, since the majority of their buying decisions are emotional.

I consistently teach this concept in all aspects of the

sales cycle.

We must connect with our clients on an emotional level and then utilize that connection to solve logical problems. Therefore, before going into the plan, I try to touch on some emotional pieces we discussed during the fact-finder interview.

For example, if you talked about the client's goals for retirement – and if you've followed my teachings in the fact-finder chapter – you will fully understand that person by hearing their story. That story will be on personal feelings related to childhood experiences or perhaps adult experiences involving parents, grandparents, in-laws, etc.

Let's use a hypothetical scenario where the clients informed us they wanted to retire at age 65, with an annual income of $200,000 until age 85. In the introduction, I would remind them of the old IRAs on their balance sheet, their current 401(k), their contribution, the company's matching contribution, and the current balances.

However, I would not stop there. Following the introduction, I might add details offered about their goals.

"Remember, Mr. Prospect, you went pretty deep into telling me about both your in-laws' and parents' situations, and you mentioned how enjoyable your in-laws' retirements are due to the planning and work they put into it throughout their careers. You also stated quite the opposite about your own parents. You mentioned how financial uncertainties have affected their house and your relationships with your siblings, specifically, regarding who is currently stepping up to help them. Last but not least, you mentioned the critical importance of living in retirement like your in-laws, not your parents."

That approach is a vital part of the introduction, because if I effectively used the information I gathered from the fact-finder section, I will have connected and struck a chord with the client about their parents' past failures. By connecting at this level, the client realizes how critically important it is to not repeat those failures, with me leading the way as their financial guide.

What is the lesson here? Learn to connect via a meaningful, personal story by using the gift of seeking to understand emotional issues before presenting logical solutions to the client's gaps. More often than not, our clients know they have inadequate areas of their plan that they don't need us to highlight in a meeting. Instead, they need to feel that we understand and care about them and that we can hold their hand through a lifelong journey to financial security. We accomplish this by initially seeking to understand and connect with them on an emotional level, so they are much more open to the logical solutions we deliver later in the process. Therefore, those emotional touches are absolutely necessary in the introduction.

The next important part of the introduction is to help clients understand that you did your best job by asking all the necessary questions, listening to their responses, and gathering precisely accurate information. The entire process of the plan presented to them will help them better understand the steps necessary to achieve their financial goals.

This is a crucial stage because many clients assume that the financial advisor intends to use a plan to manipulate them to buy something they don't need. Stated another way, my kind of plan is developed through strategies the advisor feels are important for the *client*, as opposed to the other way around.

We provide clarity to clients by saying, "Listen, this plan is not based on my values or opinions, nor is it based on textbook statistics. What you're about to see is based on the numbers you've provided and the things you told me that would be important for your financial security."

The last part of the introduction should simply help them understand the broad topics you're going to discuss. The most common topics I deal with in the planning process include survivor income, disability income, college education planning, and retirement planning. (When we work with senior clientele, long-term care planning becomes an important topic to add to the discussion.)

In summary, an effective introduction will inform the clients about the meeting's purpose, while clearly illustrating their financial situation in a manner that speaks to them emotionally as well as logically, to demonstrate that you have truly listened to them and understand their situation.

Once you've established clarity, you can use the analogy that you're simply there to hold up a mirror to them to show what it will take to achieve their most important financial goals. Also inform them that your planning comes from the perspective that they eventually earn an "A" grade in every single category.

To wrap up your intro, describe the overall areas you will cover, so your clients have an idea of the discussion before you open the first page of the plan.

———————————— ————————————

Based on my financial philosophy, it is of critical importance in both my practice and teaching that we address *crisis* management *first* with our clients, even before wealth accumulation planning.

The basis for my philosophy is that clients who save for their children's college without addressing insurance needs are unlikely to realize their financial goals, especially in the event of an untimely death.

Conversely, if we *start* with life insurance and subsequently add educational planning, we follow a path that I believe makes clients nearly bulletproof. That plan postulates that if they live long enough, they will accumulate ample money through planning, and, even in the event of death or disability, their children will have access to college funds.

Thus, the first section I address in my plan is the survivor income section.

Addressing the Need for Life Insurance

Before going into the survivor income section, I help clients understand the fundamental purpose of buying life insurance. I start by telling them what it is *not* intended to do: to make a widow wealthy. Some people joke about being worth more dead than alive, saying that, with a large life insurance policy, their spouse would be better off. Although that might (or might not) be funny, it's nowhere near the truth when you're doing the work necessary for financial security.

I help clients understand that the best reason for them to buy life insurance is to maintain their lifestyle. I explain to them that my wife and I enjoyed an enviable lifestyle in our 20s. But as my business grew and we continued to enhance our lifestyle into our mid-30s, we would have been emotionally crushed if a financial setback had forced us to return to our lifestyle of a decade earlier. But, thanks to sound financial planning, if I had had an untimely death in my mid-30s, I was secure in the knowledge that my family would not have had to revert to our earlier lifestyle.

When your clients gain that perspective, I think it truly sets in that they're on a meaningful path.

Regarding survivor income, we must begin with what we're trying to accomplish in the event that they don't make it home one night. I make my approach perfectly clear by saying, "Mr. Prospect, these are the income numbers you told me would be important to you." I then mention that many clients ask, "What is the right amount of life insurance for my income?" I answer that there is no magic formula for the proper amount; it's the amount a person requires to do what's important for them to do. I add, "That's why I hung in there and asked so many questions last week to find out what was important to you. These numbers that we're looking at are the numbers that you gave me."

I also want them to know that basic survivor income planning is broken down into three components. These components include the following in no particular order:

- elimination of debt
- funds set aside to pay for education
- replacement of an income stream for a lengthy period that is desirable to your client

Other survivor income uses include philanthropic, family foundations, estate tax planning, and so on, but the three bulleted above are the most generic and basic for most clients.

Before getting into details, I remind them of all the areas this plan will *not* cover for their surviving spouse. It's critical that the client understands that if we buy the amount of life insurance stated in the plan, their spouse will be able to get by, but will likely have to endure a tremendous amount of sacrifice. For instance, the plan amount does not include funds for additional home repairs or for new car purchases or other unforeseen expenses. They are simply planning to freeze the current lifestyle and continue it for a certain period of years.

I then go through the plan, beginning with the easy parts, as follows.

The client currently has X amount of debt – let's say

$300,000. We want to pay that off (as they said previously), so that's the amount necessary to pay off their total debt.

Then, we need to evaluate the education situation. The client may have mentioned wanting, in today's dollars, $25,000 per year for four years of college tuition for each of their children. Therefore, I will walk them through this based on the cost to educate their kids, subtract what they've set aside (if any), and inform them of the present net value to fund future tuition of each child.

Next, I repeat to them the income replacement they desire, in the following manner, "Mr. Prospect, out of the $10,000 per month you live on today, you mentioned that, if the principal was paid off on your mortgage, you would want to have $7,500 a month going to your spouse for the next 20 years until age 65, and you would want it to be, in today's dollars, $5,000 per month until age 85, the life expectancy you are comfortable with."

For the next step, I guide the client through the planning charts, showing how much capital needs to be set aside to provide an income stream through a net present value discounted to a single number. I then add the same net present value single number for education and add the amount of debt they have. Those three combined values make up the total amount of capital necessary in the unfortunate event of immediate death.

Next, I subtract from that number their current assets and policies they currently have. The difference represents what they need to buy now.

Income Replacement:	$1,000,000
Education:	$200,000
Debt:	$300,000
TOTAL	**$1,500,000**
CURRENTLY OWN	**-$500,000**
TOTAL NEEDED	**$1,000,000**

Hypothetical Example. Not for Reuse.

This marks a critical point in the planning process. I believe many reps miss this point, which I refer to as *where the rubber hits the road*. Let's assume the final number totaled $1 million before proceeding. My approach might be as follows.

"Mr. Prospect, your number today, based on what we agreed you need and what you have, is $1 million. To provide for your family in the way we just reviewed, and before going any further, how do you feel about that number?"

The client's answer will largely determine where we go next. Let me offer some examples.

The first response might be, "Yes, that makes a lot of sense the way you laid it out. I've never done that before. I've never looked at it that way. Although I'm not excited about having that additional expense, I believe you've done a good job, and that's the number I need."

That might happen 5 to 10% of the time.

The other extreme might be a client responding, "I'm

not interested in buying more life insurance because the reality is I've only got X amount to invest, so we'll just have to deal with whatever happens. I'm fine."

This is where a strong relationship with your client empowers you to say:

"Mr. Prospect, once again, my job today is not to tell you what amount you need to buy in addition to what you have. My job is simply to ask good questions, listen to your answers, and use my systems and planning materials to inform you as to what you need. Having said that, the numbers are what the numbers are. You can use 10 different calculators and calculate the numbers six ways to Sunday based on your current assets, and your stated objective – $1 million – is the amount you need now. We don't have to do that, but in my practice, I just want to be 100% certain that we've identified the right amount. So, before we proceed, let's go back to the education. Let's go back to the income replacement and the timeframe you want the income replaced, let's figure out if and where you feel comfortable lowering those numbers, and let's get to the right number."

And then you listen to the client's response. When a client understands that they will need to cut education funding or provide their spouse far less income, for a shorter time than needed, they usually don't truly want to do those things. I find that strategy works.

I also say:

"Mr. Prospect, I appreciate your hesitancy to own this number. After all, $1 million is a huge amount to many people. But let me share what I think is extremely important in my practice as it relates to life insurance proceeds. My job is to help you understand that I will establish a funding amount that dictates your *family's future for the rest of their lives.*"

The opposite scenario that most people think about is called a "windfall profit." Let me give you an example of this.

If you are healthy and working and happen to win the lottery, it would be a great feeling, and you'd probably want to throw a huge party to celebrate. However, if I offered you a million-dollar check with the condition that you agree never to work another day again to earn income, how would you feel about that?

More often than not, clients understand the implications of this scenario and claim they would not cash the check. But let me share this concept: If, God forbid, you don't make it home tonight and your spouse receives a check from the insurance company, your spouse is in a much different place than if they'd received a windfall profit.

Next, I inform my clients that if they don't smoke and are in good health, term life insurance is relatively inexpensive and often equal to, or sometimes less than, their car insurance. I urge them to not be too hung up on this, and if we go the least expensive route, it's probably no more than current car insurance payments. I finally encourage them to take a deep breath, and they usually feel much better about what they're doing.

I want you to learn from this section of the planning module that by the time you conclude the survivor income section, you and your prospective client should be in sync, hand-in-hand, knowing the exact amount necessary to buy (in addition to what they already have) so they can do what's truly important. Although they might not be doing cartwheels, they should fully understand and own it.

It's only when they fully understand the situation that I'm willing to move into the next section: disability.

The Client Conversation on Disability Income

I tell clients that disability, like death, is no fun to think about. But as a financial advisor, one of my missions is to make my clients financially bulletproof, and disability insurance is a critically important aspect of their plan.

I tell them that most clients initially do not necessarily think much about disability insurance. They look at it the same way that they look at their health insurance, which they have through their employer and, therefore, feel good about their coverage.

However, as financial advisors, we all know that the group disability through an employer is better than nothing, but it's nowhere near enough to cover most monthly household financial commitments.

At this stage in my disability income planning section, I use a very simplistic approach. In a three-column spreadsheet, I use green figures in the left-hand column to illustrate the client's net monthly income (after-tax and all deductions). Let's say that figure is $10,000.

The next column, in yellow, displays the net amount coming into their household in the event of a disability, after-tax, through their employer group plan – let's say $5,500.

The third column, color-coded red, shows the shortage between their group plan and their healthy ordinary income. Hypothetically, that number is $4,500.

Disability Income

Monthly Income	Employer Group Plan	Shortage ("The Gap")
$10,000/ month	$5,500/ month	$4,500/ month

Hypothetical Example. Not for Reuse.

With that amount presented, I'd say:

"This green column is what you're making now. In the event of a disability, this yellow column is what your household would receive, and therefore this red column is the Gap, which I see as a concern. Tell me before I move forward: How do you feel about that?"

This is another area in the planning module where the rubber hits the road. This is an absolute no-brainer. My goal is to make every one of my clients bulletproof, and I know that if they don't have adequate disability coverage, I must help them understand a vital fact: *disability is more likely than premature death.* This fact can shock and upset them, but that kind of emotional response to the facts can propel them into action.

I may break in here and tell clients that there will be numerous components of the plan that are fun and exciting to discuss, but those come only after we hit our basic goals. I show empathy at this point by acknowledging that disability insurance is not fun, it's more of a necessary evil. It's as important as homeowner's insurance or car insurance, which most people have, so I help them understand my conviction on this matter.

I also make clear that there are other problem areas in their disability planning besides the Gap in the graphs I highlighted. I inform them that most group plans have no index for inflation, so in the event of a long-term disability, the purchasing power of the dollar from their benefit will go down every year.

I also help them understand that most group disability does not cover beyond six months the cost of medical insurance, and I discuss the added cost of that aspect. Furthermore, I talk to them about having no contributions to retirement plans so, in the event of a long-term disability not impacting life expectancy, their life beyond 65 suffers because the group disability goes away, resulting in inadequate retirement funds.

I cover all these aspects of the disability section before moving forward. I make it clear that by looking at their situation, it seems obvious that they should at least be educated about the definitions and costs of a supplemental disability policy. I ask if we are on the same page and then remain quiet until they confirm. Otherwise, I'm probably not going to proceed further.

I must then address any issues or questions they have. One example might be: "Jim, I'm a lawyer. I work at my desk. If I were disabled, I could just come to work because it's not like I'm laying concrete. So, that's not really a concern of mine."

That would be an instance of an individual not relating to the real potential of a devastating disability. I would reply to the client:

"Mr. Prospect, I can understand and appreciate your position. I work almost exclusively in a white-collar world. Many of my clients feel the same way when we first meet. Having said that, let me ask you a question: When did you last have a 103° temperature or a bad case of the flu that prevented you from working?"

Posed that question, they quickly understand that, in the event of disability, whether it is a mild sickness or cancer, the last place they want to be is at their workplace. I simply remind them that great planning is all about having options. My job is to make sure you don't have to go to work feeling miserable. With a small disability insurance premium, the option exists. Most of my clients grasp the concept when described to them in this manner.

The Art of Education Planning

The next section is education. I begin the education section with the following summary:

"Mr. Prospect, we're now going into education and will look at what's necessary to fully fund your kids' education the way that you explained it to me last week. However, it's important for you to understand that, like the other sections, education planning is an art, not a science. I realize inflation rates have greatly increased education costs over the last several decades, and I factored that into this plan. But that doesn't necessarily mean that's what education will cost over the next 15 years. We don't know for sure whether your child will go to college, or receive scholarships, or what aid will be available. However, by carefully reviewing this plan and starting to think into the future as it relates to your kids' education, you'll be in a much better spot than most Americans who refuse to plan early. Once again, we will create several options for you down the road."

I teach clients that if they set aside X amount of college tuition dollars, but things don't work out as they expect – maybe they never reach the point of fully funding tuition, or their child opts to not attend college or earns scholarship funding – possessing too much money for the college years is preferable to not enough. Before jumping into the education analysis with clients, I also make it a point to discuss alternative means of covering college costs.

The reason I do this is twofold. First, I believe in the deepest part of my heart that clients buy things they perceive as different, as new, and as attractive (remember the emotional component of which I mentioned earlier). Financial advisors rarely offer alternative methods of funding college education other than from drawing upon accumulated personal assets.

Let's face it: Without your help, 90% of your clients will not have ample assets to pay for their kid's education, but 90% of those clients' kids will go to school anyway. In short, college will have a major financial consequence on the family, and I believe it's our role to fully address this issue. For instance, if the client has a spouse at home, one option is the spouse returning to work when the children reach college age. I want to know if they've discussed this option with the spouse, as well as their spouse's earning potential and the likelihood of that happening.

I also discuss how parents sometimes borrow money to pay for school, often through home equity loans. I talk to clients about the dangers of home equity loans, along with the financial jeopardy these loans mean for their retirement planning.

I explain how a child can borrow money. I inform the client that it's important to put *retirement planning before education planning*. I sometimes joke that I've never seen an individual fill out an application for a retirement loan because they don't exist. Students, on the other hand, constantly apply for loans, so if we drop one ball here, it's best to be on the education front, since there are always alternative options.

Next, I attempt to educate clients – in three minutes or

less – about how student loans work, the different types of government student loans available, how and when to apply, where current interest rates stand, how long they will have to pay off student loans, and what penalties they may face in the event of delinquency for a cosigned student loan. I do this because I care. I also want my clients to know that I know my stuff.

Then I go through the educational analysis in the plan. I use the number that they told me they want in today's dollars per year. I have the birthdates of each of their children, so I can use historical college education inflation rates to show the cost in future dollars. I then show their current assets and whether they are currently contributing to it on a regular basis. I add that in and, at the end of the process, present the entire amount of capital necessary, discounted back to net present value, required to educate their children. Next, I detail the value of all their current accounts and show them the Gap between the two.

For example, for two children, let's say the lump sum Gap today totals $70,000. I explain to the client what they need to pay per year, broken down by child in order to fill that $70,000 Gap. At the end of that explanation, I want to create some sort of emotional connection. Most often, clients realize the cost of education is a big, scary number and that it's almost unachievable without knowing exactly what it is.

So, I might say the following:

"Remember, Mr. Prospect, in our fact-finding meeting, you told me the number you thought education would be was scary, but you never knew the exact number and how enlightening it would be to know. Although you might not really want to know the truth, you acknowledged it would be helpful if you could understand what it takes to save every year to fully fund both your children at the rate that you want. You told me that in our last meeting. Now that we've gone through this plan, you have your number. So, I just want to ask you: How do you feel about that?"

You now have a meaningful, emotional dialogue around which to build a relationship between you and the client, the likes of which the client has never experienced before.

This is an area where we must also have empathy. Clients might have a deep desire to educate their kids, but when they see the number necessary to pay for college, they come to the realization that it's simply not possible with their present plan.

It's at that point we want to help them understand that doing something is better than doing nothing. The feeling they will get from their children getting to college and the feeling they will get from financially contributing to that achievement is a much better feeling than contributing nothing. And it's never too late to start.

I also point out to clients that I provide education planning on a daily basis, and rarely are clients able to fully fund their kid's entire education.

Planning for the Retirement Road Ahead

Now we go into retirement. Once again, as with the beginning of the other sections, we inform clients that this is an art, not a science.

If our client is a 35-year-old, we let them know that we put the figures in for them to retire at 65, and 30 years is a long time away. We explain that we don't know what taxes or inflation rates will be for those 30 years, and, therefore, we can't predict the rate of return over that period. However, an educated guess will help us do a much better job of planning than if we simply ignore the future and do nothing at all. The other concept I convey to clients is that it's truly a gift to be able to think about retirement at such a young age.

At this point, I offer an analogy that aids clients in understanding that, as they begin the journey of building their retirement future, they're actually building an engine. If we use a generic retirement planning formula of 40 years, a young man or woman starting at age 25 and working until age 65, they have 40 years to build that engine. Once they retire at 65, that engine fuels their retirement lifestyle for the rest of their life. But *they only get one chance to build that engine.*

It's a powerful analogy if I'm dealing with a 35-year-old. I say, "You probably don't look at it this way, but do you realize that 25% of the time you have to build your retirement engine is already behind you and you can never get that back? The good news is 75% remains, and we can make up for lost time. This is a great time to start thinking about retirement planning, and often people wait far too long."

Before diving into the numbers, I explain that the following section will show what's necessary for them to retire at age 65, at (for example) $200,000 of income, adjusted for inflation, until their 85th birthday.

"Now, Mr. Prospect, the number I'll show you represents your definition of what it's going to take to attain your goals, but I also want you to understand that there are alternative options to retirement planning if that's not totally achievable."

I want to walk them through those options, as I did in college planning. I might say, "You could work longer. Who's to say you have to retire at age 65? That's obviously an option in this analysis, and it's achievable. If we have you working until age 70, the amount that you need to start saving now is substantially lower."

Second, I offer them the option of working on a part-time basis after 65 to supplement the Gap.

Furthermore, the situation may dictate that I point out to the client that the $200,000 goal they gave me is simply wishful thinking. I explain to them that we can always go back and lower that number, along with lowering lifestyle expectations.

Finally, I tell them that I put together a conservative rate of return in the analysis because I prefer retirement *not* be a gamble. However, we can have a more aggressive approach in their investments and therefore put a higher level of expectation of rate of return, but I will walk them through all those options.

I simply assist the client to understand the lump sum amount of money needed in today's dollars to deliver that $200,000 a year income. I help them understand the future value of all their current retirement savings at age 65, including the current 401(k) to which they're contributing and their employer is matching.

I show the client the Gap, by superimposing the amount of assets it takes to deliver that income, compared to the amount of assets needed if they change nothing, resulting in the Gap at age 65. Let's say for now that Gap is $1,500,000. Therefore, I demonstrate at age 35, based on a certain rate of return on their investments, how much they need to save each year, starting today, so that by age 65 they will add an additional $1.5 million to their current assets.

Then I stop and state:

"You know, we just covered a lot, but basically we covered what you need to do in order to get what you want out of retirement. You need to continue doing what you're doing with your current employer's 401(k), plus we need to hope that there are no reductions to that plan. On top of that, you need to save an additional X thousands of dollars each month on your own, so every year you can continue to build the engine bigger. Before I go any further, how do you feel about this?"

This is another area where the rubber hits the road for the client. You know how truly interested they are based on their level of being what I call "professionally disturbed." This is analogous to a substantially overweight individual coming to grips with the fact that they must change their diet and start exercising.

It's at that point that you can figure out whether these are crucial goals for the client, or just wishful thinking. It's the same with virtually every client. Are they committed to making some sacrifices to save an extra thousand dollars a month, or was the retirement plan they gave you essentially a pipe dream?

It's impossible in this book to provide you a path for all possible conversations based on how clients react, but you must go down the various paths they take with them, and listen and help them find the way to financial success in the long run. The worst outcome is for a client to not believe the numbers you gave them, or to be unwilling to deal with it and ask you to just move on. That means you're following the analysis of your plan from logic alone – and that you, the financial planner, are unwilling to take the heightened level of interpersonal risk to connect with the client emotionally.

The truth of the matter is that very few clients will step up and follow your advice without your guidance. They must understand that they can indeed make sacrifices and that a good plan is all about progress, not necessarily perfection. Just like many of us didn't earn straight "A"s in every class, getting a "B" or "B+" or "B-" in financial planning is not the end of the world. If this client can start with $500 a month and work their way up, you're helping them in an amazing way. We want them to feel good about that, and we want to be able to hone in on that positive feeling before we leave.

The Financial Planning Checklist

The next section details what I call the financial planning checklist. People love visuals. My checklist has approximately 11 boxes, from having adequate liquid cash, to funding retirement, to funding education, to having a will. At the end of the plan, I like to show them all the different things that they need to have in order to be completely financially secure.

Then, I want to show them where they would be on that checklist if they follow my recommendations.

Finally, I want to show them where they are on the checklist right now if they do nothing. This visual helps them understand that, even if they do everything you're currently recommending, which people rarely do, there's still much work to be done until they ultimately achieve financial security.

I help them see that getting a check in every one of the boxes on the list equates to a 30- or 40-year journey, and I explain that it's my job to put my arm around them and walk side-by-side with them during the journey, on a relentless pursuit to checking off every single box.

I like to use this checklist for all the reasons I've stated, but also for my annual reviews, to demonstrate the progress we are making together each year and illustrate that there is light at the end of the tunnel.

The Financial Planning Checklist

☐ Client has the right amount of life insurance

☐ Client has the right kind of life insurance

☐ Client has sufficient amount of disability insurance

☐ Client has sufficient amount of long-term care insurance

☐ Client has adequate amount of short-term liquidity

☐ Client has eliminated all unnecessary debt

☐ Client has the most efficient college savings accounts set up

☐ Client has the most adequate amount of funding to support future college costs

☐ Client has adequate amount of retirement assets along with a plan for current funding to achieve their goal

☐ Client assets are allocated appropriately to be in alignment with their risk profile

☐ Client has adequate amount of estate planning completed

This is a great point in the planning meeting to discuss prioritization. When clients look at what you suggested they need to do and they review the entire checklist of what needs to be done for financial security, it doesn't take them long to figure out that reaching total financial security right then and there is virtually impossible.

For example, let's assume after the four components of planning that you've created an individual plan where it's necessary that they: invest in an additional $1.5 million of life insurance, buy $4,000 a month of extra supplemental disability insurance, save $750 a month for their kids' education, and save an additional $1,000 a month for retirement.

Thus, without the cost of disability or life insurance, they need to save an additional $750 to $1,750 per month just for education and retirement goals.

However, you know based on their income and preliminary conversations that their budget today is $500 a month, at best. It's at this point that you must have a conversation where a big role you play as the client's advisor is to help them *prioritize their planning* and make certain that they are at least taking steps in the right direction – that there is a method to the plan and a light at the end of the tunnel. Your job is to connect with them and hold their hand throughout the next 20, 30, or 40 years to reach total security.

At the beginning of this planning chapter, I explained that I start out by helping clients understand my philosophy. The reason I go through survivor income and disability is that I believe we must take care of risk management first, before working on wealth accumulation.

For what I perceive to be obvious reasons, when we prioritize, I help clients understand that I follow a disciplined philosophy, which calls for addressing $1.5 million of life insurance and $4,000 per month supplemental disability right out of the gate. If we accomplish that in the least expensive way, we may still have some additional capital for college and/or retirement planning, while emphasizing retirement planning prior to college, simply because we can't take loans for lack of retirement funds. Once I've had that conversation and we are on the same page, I move to the final stage of the planning process.

The last stage of the planning process is the transition language. The transition language is vital. Here's why: An important part of your skill set is the ability to present the plan in a simple, accessible way without leaving out any content. This will come with thoughtful preparation, practicing your plan delivery, and by using clear and simple language when talking with the prospect.

Hypothetically, if we look at the planning meeting, let's say it requires 90 minutes to cover all four of these sections. By that point, the average prospect's head will be spinning. This is not information they deal with on a daily basis, and they can easily become confused and overwhelmed.

Hence, the purpose of the transition language is to use, what I often preach, my three Cs: being concise, clear, and compelling. And we want to do this in no more than three to four minutes.

So, after we've covered everything in the plan, we need to say, "Boy, we've covered a lot today, and I want to thank you for being attentive. But, I also realize that sometimes my clients can be overwhelmed. So, with your permission, I'd like to do an executive summary of what we covered over the last hour and a half."

Since clients always agree to an executive summary, we need to be able to *briefly* review what we've told them: "Here's what we looked at and concluded in the survivor income section."

Then we should add a few emotional touches, which might sound like this, "We concluded X number, Mr. Prospect, and when I asked you how you felt about it, you told me that, before we met today, never in a million years would you think you'd have that much insurance. But, based on the way I educated and led you through it, you looked at the numbers and the way it's calculated, and told me you totally understand it and appreciated my thoroughness."

I go back and walk the client through what we learned in the disability section, followed by retirement planning, then education planning.

Next, I sum up and say:

"Mr. Prospect, what we have learned up until this point is that in order to get an 'A' in your comprehensive financial plan, we would need to accomplish the following: We would need an additional $1.5 million in life insurance, an additional $4,000 per month disability policy, increase our retirement savings by $1,000 per month, and increase our college savings accounts by $750 per month. When you hear me sum this up, what thoughts come to mind?"

First, we have to be certain that the client is on the same page with everything we covered. Second, we want to get to the heart of the emotional aspect because they know they only have X amount of dollars, far less than what you told them they need. This is where we can show empathy with our clients and help them understand our overall philosophy – that it's about progress, not perfection, and the sooner we start doing something, the far better off we are than if we do nothing.

Prior to going through the executive summary, I want every one of my students to say to the client, "The next time we get together, my job is to show you the solutions to the gaps that we covered today. It's imperative that you and I are on the same page as to what those gaps are, so the next time we meet we're singing the same tune to solve them."

You can use whatever language you want, but what I'm trying to teach here is the critical importance of the client understanding that when they leave the planning meeting, first and foremost, they have some gaps (you can call them "problems" or whatever you like). Regardless, the client definitely has gaps, and they must recognize them and take complete ownership of them. Based on your style, you will have built a level of "professional disturbance" around those gaps and created a desire to solve them.

It's also imperative that they know exactly what you're going to do in the next meeting, which is giving them the most economically efficient, creative, and comprehensive solutions to solve the problems you mutually spent an hour and a half uncovering.

To the extent the client understands these problems, solving them becomes a necessity, not an option. The only question is how to solve them. That gives you the advantage of not coming back as a "salesman selling them a product," but as *their number-one financial advocate* whom they now rely upon to help them get to where they so passionately want to be.

This planning meeting is always fun to teach to my students. I believe it represents a huge shift in the industry. I also believe the reps who strive to do well in this regard will create the perception that they're there for the clients, as opposed to being mere salesmen pitching products. They view themselves as participants in a lifelong journey that they are committed to completing with the client. They make their clients start to feel comfortable, and the first way they demonstrate that relationship is through the planning meeting.

Summing up a somewhat controversial issue, I am highly opposed to bringing any kind of products and closing the client at the end of the planning meeting. I want to make sure my clients understand these are two separate meetings. The planning meeting is designed to uncover the problems, and the closing meeting is designed to solve them. I believe the meetings should remain completely separate. I want to make sure that, when I leave a planning meeting, the client completely owns their problems. But, I also want to build a desire for them to want me to come back to begin to solve those problems because I've created a level of discomfort that they realize they have these issues that must be solved.

SYSTEM FOR PLANNING

1. Begin with an executive summary of what was covered in the fact-finding meeting.
2. In each section of the plan, connect with clients on an emotional level.
3. Use consistent planning pages that are broken down into the following categories: survivor income, disability income, college education, and retirement income.
4. Provide a mini-summary at the end of each section.
5. Anticipate and prepare for common challenges from clients.
6. Take notes on changes to the plan that need to be made.
7. At the conclusion of the planning meeting, summarize the plan, prioritize gaps that need to be addressed, set expectations for the next meeting, and schedule the next meeting.

BRIDGE YOUR GAP • JIM EFFNER

BRIDGE YOUR GAP • JIM EFFNER

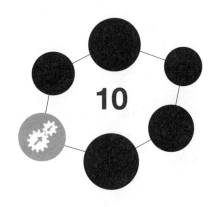

IMPLEMENTATION

As you enter the implementation stage – and, by the way, some financial representatives call this the "closing stage" of the sales cycle – it is imperative to begin the meeting with language that brings the client completely back to where you left off the prior meeting. Let me make myself clear once again: I am adamant about holding separate meetings for planning and implementation.

As I stated earlier, it's not only overwhelming to the client to go over both in the same meeting, it also requires an entirely different mindset to achieve total buy-in. Therefore, from a psychological standpoint, I believe it is imperative to separate the two.

Once again, the planning meeting's purpose is to take the client's goals and objectives and hold up a mirror to show them the problems in their plan.

The purpose of the implementation meeting is to use your creative intellectual horsepower to offer solutions for closing the gaps identified in the planning meeting. As stated in the planning module, if the client doesn't take total ownership of those problems, you don't stand a chance in hell of closing them in the implementation meeting.

You now reach the implementation stage with the assumption that the client is disturbed and owns the problems you pointed out in the previous meeting. How you open this meeting is important. Let's assume that it's been somewhere between 10 days and two weeks since the planning meeting, and you come back today to present ideas to close the Gap.

I often explain to the client, "Mr. or Mrs. Prospect, I'm not naïve enough to feel as if the only thing you've thought about since our last meeting was our plan. I know you've had family events and work. You have your social life and everything else, so if you don't mind, I'd like to open up with an executive summary of what we concluded in our last meeting so, as I proceed, I'm certain you and I are on the same page. Fair enough?"

I previously mentioned presenting an executive summary. If you go back to the first time I taught this at the end of the fact-finder chapter, I discussed a discovery agreement – a three- or four-minute executive summary of what you learned in the fact-finder meeting. The discovery agreement applies the "three Cs": clear, concise, and compelling. When you reconnect with the client at the planning meeting, provide an executive summary of that discovery agreement. Then, at the end of the planning meeting, give another executive summary before leaving and, before beginning the implementation stage, offer yet another executive summary in your opening language.

This strategy is important for many reasons. First, it gives the client an eloquently stated summary, in both your phrasing and the three Cs: clear, concise, and compelling. They start to internalize it and, therefore, own it. It becomes their problem. Second, they have clarity as to the purpose and, therefore, know exactly what you have mutually agreed upon regarding the problems. Additionally, they know what you're there to discuss in terms of how to solve their problems. Finally, I believe effective summaries help clients understand an overwhelming amount of information. In other words, a financial rep who summarizes well can help clients understand an otherwise rather complex topic.

Thus, with this opening language, strive to summarize all areas covered in the planning meeting. Let's say you completed a traditional planning document that covered a client's life insurance needs, disability insurance needs, retirement savings goals, and education savings goals. Your opening statement should be an executive summary of each of those compartments. At the end of that opening statement, you must ask if what you explained made sense to them, if you missed anything, and if they would like to add anything. This is when they give you permission to proceed and confirm that they are on the same page as you.

Remember here that it is extremely important to be concise without eliminating any critical information. If your clients requested changes after the planning meeting, this opening is also a great time to acknowledge that you heard them and that you made those changes.

For example, let's assume that the client originally gave you a goal of providing for, in today's dollars, $30,000 per year per child for education. However, after they realized the monumental savings necessary, they wanted to talk it over with their spouse. They concluded that the goal is to pay only $20,000 per year, with their children paying the remaining balance. During the summary, you want to inform them that you made those changes.

It is also important to personalize your summary. Remember, as I've taught throughout this book, the biggest mistake financial reps make is assuming this is a logical business. It's not. It's an emotional business, and we must connect with our clients, which you can accomplish through clear, concise, and compelling summaries.

For example, in the planning meeting, assume you discussed how much a client needed to exceed the 401(k) contribution to hit their retirement goals. Until now, they haven't developed the discipline to do so. When you unveiled that in the planning meeting, they were a little overwhelmed by how much they would need to save on top of the 401(k). They also told you how important it was because they watched their parents deteriorate from stress during their retirement due to poor planning.

In your summary, you could reference this as follows:

"Mr. or Mrs. Prospect, if you remember in the retirement section, above and beyond your 401(k), we learned that you need to save an extra thousand dollars a month for your retirement. You mentioned that that was a staggering number to you and also shared with me the relevancy of it based on what you've experienced with your parents."

Doing this demonstrates to the client that you listened and understood – and that you care. Reminding them of the discussion also helps them connect the significant desire through their emotions and their own story so they can act. Conversely, logic alone would not create the momentum to do so.

It's very important at the end of the summary to ask if you covered everything thoroughly, if you left something out, or if they would like to add anything. Until you get buy-in at that point, you must not proceed.

For example, if they claim the survivor income section made sense when you explained it 10 days ago, but they have since realized they over-funded their spouse's needs, it's imperative that you say, "Tell me more about that. What sort of changes would you like me to make?" Don't be a bull in the china shop and stampede on through.

Sometimes they might agree with everything in the meeting, but a spouse who isn't present might have a different opinion.

Imagine you just walked in the door and shared a few niceties before giving your opening summary. At the end, you concluded feeling very comfortable being on the same page with the client. I believe it is important in the next stage of the implementation sales cycle for reps to begin by helping clients understand the significance of having a financial foundation.

Building the Financial Foundation

Most reps I work with have reported that this is not an issue for their clients. It could be overkill in that scenario. However, if it's an issue for your client, it's important to walk them through and explain what a financial foundation is. In no particular order, a financial foundation involves three things: owning versus renting, removing all foolish debt such as consumer debt and credit card debt, and having an adequate amount of liquidity in their savings account.

For adequate liquidity, I suggest a multiple of 3 times their monthly household budget. You want to be a "real" financial advisor at this point. If we do not address this issue, the meeting simply becomes all about you as an advisor, not truly about your client. More often than not, advisors aren't dealing with this because they receive no compensation for advice in this area.

Once again, this is a great opportunity for me to teach that your compensation should always be an ancillary benefit of putting the client first and relentlessly guiding them to the land of financial security.

Step number one for many people in this country is building the financial foundation. If they haven't accomplished this, they need your help. It's imperative that you talk to them about it. Additionally, doing so will show that you're putting their needs first, and that you truly care about doing the right thing. It will help them perceive that you are a trustworthy financial planner and advisor, as opposed to a dispassionate salesperson. When you spend time discussing these issues, your clients will realize you're not in it purely for profit, and that will earn you a tremendous amount of respect.

Finally, regarding the financial foundation, it's not only a matter of talking to your clients and educating them before moving on. You must adopt in your practice a way to help them build their foundation. For example, you could talk to them about the importance of spending on their credit cards only what they can afford for that month.

In addition, you could help them establish a monthly automatic withdrawal or savings plan that moves funds from a checking account into a savings account until it's big enough to pay off their credit card debt. Then, you could help them continue the same game plan until they have enough for a house down payment, and until they achieve adequate liquidity. This might be a four- or five-year journey with the client, but it is important. My financial philosophy is that clients can't ignore the risk-management piece until they get the financial foundation. You have to develop a way for them to do both simultaneously.

Implementing the Life Insurance Plan

As we start educating our clients on life insurance, it's important to begin with the entire amount the plan tells them that they need. For the rest of this chapter, let's assume that the client needs $1 million, and let's assume they understand this need.

The most effective way I have found to educate clients who do not understand life insurance is to start with the most simplistic term insurance ledger to help them understand how, for a very insignificant amount of premium, they can immediately eliminate the risk of dying too soon for their family.

So, I will open with, "Mr. or Mrs. Prospect, this is term insurance. It simply works like car insurance, which means as you continue to pay the premiums, there is a death benefit amount in force. Once you stop paying the premiums, that death benefit goes away. Essentially, it is like renting your life insurance coverage. The advantages of that are, for a very low cost when you're young and healthy, you can get an exorbitant amount of death benefit to protect the young family in its early stages."

I recommend educating clients on the disadvantages of term insurance. For instance, over a long-term period beyond 30 or 40 years, term insurance is a truly expensive way to own life insurance. In addition, only 7 to 8% of all term insurance policies in the industry ever pay a death benefit. People live beyond when it becomes affordable, so they drop it long before they pass away.

I like to start with this explanation because when clients see a number like $1 million in the plan, it tends to paralyze them a bit. If they haven't dealt with that before, they feel as if it's a very big number. However, when they see the term insurance premium, especially with decreased rates and premiums as mortality tables have gone down, I think it takes a lot of stress and anxiety off their mind because it costs far less than what they expected. I believe this gives them relief and helps them understand that they can take care of a relatively big problem with an insignificant amount of money.

Then I like to take the client to the opposite extreme and run the entire amount in my company's most popular traditional permanent life insurance policy. Each company has its own favorite. For example, some companies might prefer a variable life policy, a universal life policy, or a whole life policy. I find that every company in the industry has a go-to permanent product they really love. I recommend you start with that. I provide my clients a presentation and walk them through every detail of the permanent life insurance policy. More importantly, I highlight the benefits of having permanent insurance.

At this point, I want to stress that one of the biggest mistakes reps make when going through some form of permanent ledger is describing the product in too much detail. My friends and fellow reps, if you don't already understand that life insurance is a complex product, it's about time you start admitting that.

The last thing you want to do is approach it like a pop quiz, giving them a list of facts and figures. It's like the old saying: Most individuals don't want to know how the watch is made; they want to know what time it is. Most clients don't care about the intricate details of how permanent life insurance works; they want to know why people buy it. Therefore, it is imperative that others are going over the life insurance ledger you're discussing, highlighting the client benefits as opposed to the fine details.

I also like to spend a tremendous amount of time throwing in various bullet points as to why most of my clients buy permanent insurance. A few highlighted examples include:

- the guaranteed rate of return
- the high level of fixed income in the portfolio as opposed to the whole 401(k) being in equities
- the tax advantages of the cash value build-up
- the savings discipline of having to make the premium payment every year
- the premium waiver benefit feature – if they become disabled, the company pays the premium; in fact, this is the only self-funded retirement savings vehicle in the event of a disability
- most importantly, the peace of mind of having life insurance when they die

With this last point, I conclude by saying the biggest reason my clients buy this permanent product is because, whether they are 30, 40, 50, or 90, they want some level of life insurance in force when they die, and no other insurance product on the planet delivers that unless you buy a permanent product.

As I describe the benefits and reason my clients buy different products, I subtly watch their body language. Their unspoken clues inform me as to whether they're concerned about certain issues, whether they believe their wellbeing is important to me too, and whether these are good reasons to buy the product. I am also educating them about why my other clients have made similar decisions.

Finally, I'll also march further down the road. I'll play an informative game with the client, saying, "You know what, Mr. Prospect? You're 35 today. Let's go out to age 65. You know, I think a lot of reps make mistakes when they look at permanent life insurance as a vehicle during the accumulation stage, Mr. Prospect. With my clients, I also like to help them understand permanent life insurance in its distribution stage, so let's just assume that you buy this product today. We snap our fingers and 30 years go by. You are no longer 35. Now you're 65 years old. Let's take a look at all the different features that this policy has and all the different options you will have at that time of your life. I want to make sure that you really understand."

Then, I explain pension optimization and the ability to earn tax-free income from it. I talk about the ability to freeze the death benefit and take the dividend income, lowering the death benefit to whatever level they want, surrendering paid-up insurance to create more cash, and withdrawing a large distribution. I discuss many other variables as well. I want them to understand the benefits of having us at age 65.

When finished, I simply say, "Like most good things in life, you can see that, if this is something that you really want, you can't snap your fingers on your 65th birthday and have those wonderful benefits. You have to start now at 35 to have all the perks when you are 65."

I want them to be clear about the benefits. I help them understand that it's based on mortality cost, which is based on age and health. I also help them understand the magic of compounding interest and the benefits of being in a contract for 30+ years. All of those things are important.

At this stage, the client understands that inexpensive term insurance is a short-term solution. I help them understand permanent life insurance and all the benefits in a very proactive salesmanship-type way.

Then, I end by looking at them and saying, "Now, I understand money doesn't grow on trees, but if money were not an issue whatsoever, which one of these two products would you buy and why?" Their answer is everything moving forward. A small percentage of clients will say they would obviously buy permanent insurance, but they can't afford it. If they answer this way, then you know they are on the same page as you.

However, very rarely does that happen. The other 85 to 90% of clients offer an answer indicating you must address some issues in order to agree to purchase any level of permanent insurance. Those things could be that they'd rather buy the term and invest the difference because they feel better about that. They might not see the need for life insurance beyond retirement once they are "self-insured."

They could give you a number of other objections, so you must excel at being able to respond, "You know what, Mr. Prospect? Many of my other clients felt that way when they first met me. However, I feel that once I'm able to help them understand whatever they have questions about, they do it differently. That's why I have so many successful clients who own a boat-load of permanent insurance."

If the client doesn't raise any objections, and the meeting proceeds far too smoothly, I think it's critical to mention issues. You might say, "It doesn't seem like you have any concerns, but let me tell you a couple of the most popular concerns with my clients. Sometimes they feel they can buy a term life insurance policy and invest the difference to do better. Let me tell you why that's not true."

You can come up with an objection if they don't. I strongly encourage that, as it's important when discussing permanent life insurance for clients to understand the difference between a short-term, a medium-term, and a long-term investment. You can do this by drawing a circle and then dividing it into thirds. Inside the circle, I write: "Short-term, 0 to 5 years," "Medium-term, 5 to 20 years," and "Long-term, 20 and beyond." I help them understand that nobody invests their money in a CD, a checking account, or a savings account for long-term investments. Similarly, nobody buys life insurance for a need that comes in two or three years. Every asset carries a risk, but if you place them in the appropriate timeframe, you can minimize that risk.

This is an important topic when covering permanent insurance, since understanding appropriate timeframes helps clients eliminate the objection that it takes too long to make the investment worthwhile. When advisors in any realm of the industry look at asset classes, investing, and managing money, they commonly spend 100% of the time on the accumulation stage, until the point the client retires. I think this factor is important and certainly a major aspect in which to educate your clients. I argue that it is even more important to help them understand the distribution stages as well.

Again, I like to play an educational game with my clients: "Okay, now let's assume you're 65. Let's make up a scenario of what is most likely to happen, and then look at this life insurance policy so you can understand what your options would be. I want you to be able to unwind."

Next, I walk them through paying the premiums continuously until they die, because they won't need any money; though they will have a policy with a great deal of cash in it, they will have plenty of other assets. I explain that they could freeze the death benefit of whatever the paid-up policy benefit is and take the dividend off it every year for life but retain the death benefit. I also talk about how they can cash it all in, detailing the tax laws so that they can profit without tax liability. Additionally, I talk to them about having some level of dividend income turned into an annuity. Overall, I sincerely want them to understand the post-retirement benefits and how to withdraw their money.

Bringing the Disability Plan to Life

As we move on to disability insurance, I have a story to share that molded my perspective on disability. I ended up selling a high volume of disability in my career – not for recognition or additional compensation, but because of this story.

In my first 18 months in the business, I happened to go to lunch with a veteran rep that I respect. My scheduled lunch meeting had canceled, and I wanted to pick his brain. I poked my head in his office, and he was generous enough to give me some of his time. When we sat down, I could tell he was in a funk as he looked at me and said, "Jimmy, I want to share something with you because I hope it never happens to you. I was walking in my office this morning, and the phone rang. I never answer my phone – my assistant always does, but she'd stepped out for a minute. Something came over me and told me to answer the phone, so I did. It was a very, very good client of mine who gives me a substantial amount of premium every year for life insurance and has referred me to a number of other very good clients. He proceeded to tell me that he hasn't given me an update in a while but that he had been going through a battery of tests. He was disappointed to tell me that the official diagnosis finally came back, and he was diagnosed with MS. Then, he asked me with the expectation that he and his family would be okay. He said he thought he bought this stuff called 'disability' from me, and he just wanted to make sure."

Unfortunately, my friend looked in the file and saw the caller hadn't bought disability insurance. Then he checked his case notes and realized he had never even asked the client about it. It was at this point that this rep started to tear up because he felt horrible about the oversight.

He said, "Jim, I've always prided myself in my career on making all of my clients bulletproof, and I had an opportunity to do so with a client who pretty much did everything I told him. I just didn't do my job. Don't ever put yourself in that situation."

That stuck with me for a long time. Ever since then, I made a commitment to myself to talk to every single client about disability insurance. To the extent that they chose not to take action, I would let it go, but I would make detailed notes in the case file that I did so. That way, I wouldn't feel guilty about it.

Disability is much more likely than a premature death. It's financially devastating to a family when it happens, and I believe everyone in this industry has an obligation to address it with their clients.

So, let's assume for now you discussed disability insurance in the planning meeting. The client learned in the meeting that they have a Gap in that area, and today you're simply there to close that Gap.

To begin, I say, "In our meeting last week, Mr. Prospect, we concluded that your Gap in disability was $2,500 a month. That's the amount you would need to buy in a supplemental disability policy. I know that's not something you are excited to hear, and I know there's nothing exciting about buying the product. However, I think you'll learn as I walk you through this that the premiums are minimal. However, the potential devastation to your household is quite large if you decline. I encourage you to keep an open mind as I go through it quickly and thoroughly so that you understand it."

I want to get them to the point of accepting that this is a critical thing, but I don't expect them to do cartwheels about disability insurance – any more than they would about buying car or homeowner's insurance. Still, they understand its significance, its importance, and the ramifications of not having it.

As I go through my disability ledger, I simply want them to understand that, for $2,500-a-month of disability benefit, it will cost them X dollars per month in premiums. For example, I might say, "For $2,500 a month of disability income, it will cost you $70 a month in premiums," to help them put that in perspective. I point out that, if they balk at $70 and think that's a big number, the $2,500 income Gap in the event of a disability would be insurmountable, especially if they're injured or seriously ill and can't do anything about their incapacity.

I then proceed to tell them about the benefits of individually owned disability on the ledger, which their group contract does not provide. These benefits cater to your chosen carrier, so I know it varies from company to company. The most common areas I refer to are things such as having an inflation rider and being portable if they change jobs. Some have a partial disability benefit, but I must have a better definition of disability.

For example, these policies may pay if the client can't do the job he or she was trained, educated, and experienced to perform. Most group policies simply state they pay if the client can't do any occupation. Any occupation could include being able to flip burgers at McDonald's.

Finally, you might also want to include the transition benefit. This benefit is best defined by an example. Let's say an individual makes $200,000 a year, but they become disabled for a time. At some point, their disability goes into remission, so they go back to work but still can't work as much as before. Or perhaps they can't deal with the stress of full-time work. Whatever the reason, they now only make $100,000. Even though they are no longer disabled, the transition benefit takes care of filling in that Gap in their income.

Most independent policies have a transition benefit, whereas group policies do not. This is important for them to understand. This is the Cadillac or the Mercedes of disability insurance, while a group policy is more like a Fiat.

Moving forward, I tell them that it's not just the $2,500 Gap that motivates them to do this. I remind them of the other aspects of disability that are just as imperative. I discuss losing benefits through work, losing the ability to participate in a 401(k), and losing the ability to have health insurance either at no cost or at a substantially reduced cost. I also discuss the more common scenario of increased expenses, which occur with a disability.

I end with "Mr. Prospect, I told you when we first met that the most important thing I do with my clients is I make them bulletproof. My job is not to make you rich. That is your job through your income. My job is to prevent you from ever being poor in anything that we can control. Disability is a devastating event for a family, but with the right amount of disability coverage, you can at least make sure it's not a financially devastating event as well. This is important. Is there any reason that you can't see yourself taking action with this today?"

That's how I end the disability discussion.

Executing the Retirement Plan

Now that we have completed the disability discussion, we enter into the retirement section of the plan. This client understands that, above and beyond the work programs, they need to save for, let's say, an additional $1,000 per month for their personal retirement. It's our job to come back to the meeting and concisely explain the best way to do that. I first want to help them understand every option available. I don't get paid for most of them, but I always found it earned me credibility to walk them through the options. I start by discussing their 401(k) options, suggesting we talk to their employer to determine the extent to which they can increase their 401(k) contributions, and how much additional contributions will be matched. Since that is an absolute no-brainer, I urge them to do that ASAP.

I also speak with my clients about buying individual stocks, mutual funds, or annuities with that additional money. I explain saving additional capital in a short-term liquidity account and buying real estate for rental profits. Lastly, I guide them through the process of earning supplemental retirement income from their permanent life insurance equity, based on our earlier discussion on permanent life insurance.

Furthermore, I emphasize the importance of understanding that all investments have pros and cons, no matter what any financial advisor might say. The goal of solid planning is to be able to give the client the best products for the right reasons, in the right timeframe, to minimize the associated risks. I point out that the disadvantage of the 401(k) contributions, if not matched by the employer, is the uncertainty of our country's income tax brackets when they retire. I discuss the inflexibility of taking out distributions prior to age 59½, as well as the IRS rules regarding taking distributions, whether you want them or not, after age 70½.

Finally, I explain that they still have to turn that 401(k) into income, and that there are costs associated with purchasing products that currently produce income. I never do that without also pointing out the advantages, and the fact that it lowers taxes by shielding more of their current income and offering compounded growth, which adds up over time. I also talk about the advantages, obviously, if they do match.

I do the same with stocks, mutual funds, annuities, and real estate. When the time comes to compute life insurance cash values as a retirement supplemental vehicle, I tell them there are as many advantages as disadvantages. I like to begin with the disadvantages, describing how it's a long-term commitment. If they're not willing to make a long-term commitment, it will probably hurt them more than help them. I talk to them about the attached mortality and associated charges. I even discuss the heavy upfront loads and salesman commissions, and so on, in the first, perhaps even the second year.

When it comes to advantages, I let the clients know

that owning more insurance than renting term insurance significantly lowers their overall, long-term life insurance costs. I also explain the built-in discipline of paying the premiums on a month-to-month basis. I also cover the diversification of permanent life insurance as a fixed income asset amongst other equity products, along with the guaranteed floor rate of return that comes in that company's dividend scale. I make sure to discuss the flexibility in retirement of withdrawing funds without incurring acquisition costs. I also mention that, if they don't need the funds, further enhancing their legacy or estate planning by keeping it long-term.

In short, I begin by educating them on the multiple options that I can assist with. I want to create not only the perception but also share the truth and reality that this is about doing the right thing for the client. Whatever we decide, I want the client to know I am there to help them, and I'm licensed in all of it.

I think the moral of the story is that there is no one best way to invest. Clients need to understand that diversification is important, and permanent life insurance enhances retirement as another tool in the toolbox they should take advantage of. When selling permanent life insurance with the retirement section, we must ensure we have both the philosophy and know-how to communicate in a basic, yet definitive, confident fashion.

I use a general rule with my clients, which calls for 5 to 7% of their adjusted gross income going into permanent life insurance in an ideal world. I help them understand that most of my clients must build up to that amount, and that some climb to 12 or 13% when they earn excessive income beyond their daily needs. I help them understand that everybody's different. However, when they ask me why I recommend 5 to 7%, I'm able to succinctly explain my reasons.

A few of those reasons are as follows. First, by moving 5 to 7% of their income into permanent life insurance, they can minimize their long-term insurance costs by lowering the amount they need in term insurance. The 5 to 7% is a healthy percentage that goes into a fixed income vehicle, unlike most of my clients who have always had their 401(k)s in 100% equities.

I also tell them that the standard percentages most of my clients put into their 401(k)s were 6 to 7%. The retirement goal is to save 15%, and I have found 5 to 7% in permanent life insurance is a solid supplemental vehicle to get them to the appropriate levels of savings. There are many other reasons as well, but I don't want to get too detailed in this book. What's important is forming your own philosophy, not mine, and understanding why you're recommending to a client how much permanent life insurance to buy so that it can stand the test of time, and you can back it up.

Implementing the Plan for Education Goals

I then go into the implementation meeting to discuss education. I begin by stating that, in this area of planning, my belief system says that saving for education is the last thing to do. This is because, if the client lacks adequate life insurance or disability insurance and isn't saving what they need for retirement, they really have no business saving for their kid's college education.

There are too many negative repercussions in doing so. If the children get into college without the funds for tuition, there are alternative options to help via federal student loans and so on and so forth. If the client doesn't plan appropriately for retirement, there are no loans out there that can help make up for that shortage. However, if they have their risk-management and retirement savings bases covered, it's appropriate to go through the ways in which they can save to enhance their kid's education.

Before I detail how to present this, I think it's very important – as a financial advisor who truly places clients' needs first – to help them understand what they're going to face, financially, when it comes time for their kids to go to college, regardless of whether they have a dime to save on a regular basis. I have found that only 10 to 15% of my clients have enough income to fully fund their kids' future college costs. However, virtually 100% of my clients' kids plan to attend college, and that choice will have financial implications on the household.

Therefore, this section presents an opportunity to help my clients understand that I can add value, that I really do care about them, and I want to help. So, I describe their options if they can't fully fund it on their own. I walk them through taking a home equity loan and the dangers that present, as well as why most likely that's not a good choice. You'd be amazed how many clients are planning to take a home equity loan.

When presenting the entire planning process, you can

show them the implications of a home equity loan on their retirement, and how that plays a very detrimental role. You can also explain how some married people plan on their spouse returning to work to help fund their children's college, which sometimes works. You guide your clients through situations in which others afforded private schools for their kids and thought their cash flow would pay college costs as well. Typically, I find these clients are often naïve as to the true expenses of college, so I help them understand that.

Additionally, I inform them that the most likely scenario is that their child will borrow money through government loans, so I help them understand how that process works. When the time is right to apply, I explain the necessary forms and the acquisition costs, as well as the typical interest rates and timeframes for repaying such loans. I also explain the risks and implications to the cosigner if the student defaults on payment. I have found almost 100% of the time that my clients very much appreciate that piece of information. I encourage you to have these discussions with your clients as well.

For now, let's assume that your clients have the cash flow and you spent sufficient time in the plan to help them understand the amount of money. Now it's simply a matter of walking them through one of the best educational vehicles to do so. I happen to be a huge fan of the 529 programs. That's what I used for all three of my children, so I always favor them, but I would suggest also talking with clients about whatever vehicles might be in their state and any options not in existence in my state.

Once you have all the paperwork and the program set up, closing the deal is rather simple. You let the client know that it's time to take action and that you require the first contribution. Then you set up the automatic payroll deduction or checking account withdrawal, so they can do it where it's out of sight and out of mind.

Taking Action

The final step in this implementation sales cycle is motivating your clients to take action. However, I think a very important step at this juncture is your actions as an advisor when a client lacks the funds or the discretionary cash flow to address all the issues your plan says should be addressed. I find this to be a rather controversial and stimulating topic when out in the field teaching. At this time, it's inappropriate for me to share my advice to my clients, but I urge you to do this for your own clients. You should be able to offer consistent advice that you can defend and communicate very succinctly to your clients.

As an example, let's assume the client needs $1 million life insurance and a $2,500 a month supplemental disability policy. The client also needs to save an additional $500 a month for their kids' education and an additional $1,000 a month for retirement. However, you provided a concise financial breakdown in your fact-finder meeting, and you are aware that, at best, the client has $500 a month to work with. That will likely represent 99% of your clients. Very rarely are you going to come across a client who possesses the complete amount of discretionary cash flow to cover every single problem their plan identifies. Therefore, it's important for you to be confident about what you recommend.

I cannot tell you specifically what to recommend, but I can offer how *not* to go about it. More often than not, I see reps suggesting what they think the client wants to hear. For these reps, such advice is a very subjective process, and their advice constantly changes, varying from one client to the next.

You absolutely must cease this immediately.

One of the most attractive things about working with a professional, regardless of industry, is their level of confidence in their beliefs, what they're willing to stand for, and more importantly, what they're willing to jump on a sword for. Your business is not about pleasing your clients. It's not about finding hot buttons and figuring out what they'll buy. Your business is about communicating what you believe with a tremendous level of conviction to each client and being willing to walk away from clients who disagree.

For me, it goes without saying that my priority is risk management. I help clients find the $1 million necessary for life insurance, which may initially be all term insurance. Then I suggest they buy disability insurance before we begin discussing saving money. Once they are saving, my priority shifts to retirement, then to education. I can't tell you how many challenging conversations I have had with clients far underinsured in both life and disability. These clients look at me and say, "Listen, all I want to talk about is saving money for my kids. I won't talk about anything else."

When that happens, I simply close my briefcase and move on. That's not a client that I want to work with. Knowing what you stand for and how you communicate it to your clients is imperative. Make sure you understand your position and that you can articulate it with pride and conviction.

I make clear to my clients that one of the advantages of working with me is that very few of my clients can do all of this, so it's important that they prioritize correctly. I find that my clients need a lot of help prioritizing their goals, but I can't assist them by offering a cookie-cutter approach to financial security. I must first seek to understand them – the facts, yes, but also the feelings, the story behind the human being. Once I understand them, I can draw upon my knowledge and help them prioritize based on what's important.

At this point in the meeting, having covered the plan's four sections and showing the clients every area where they need to address gaps, I start by saying:

"Well done, now let me give you a summary analysis. You need more life insurance. If you bought that on permanent life insurance, it would cost approximately $20,000 a year, and $2,500 a month of supplemental disability amounts to $1,000 a year. You need to save $500 a month or $6,000 a year for education, in addition to $1,000 a month for retirement. So, Mr. or Mrs. Prospect, if you were to do all of that, we're talking more than $40,000 a year. Obviously, that's not in your budget. I'm not going to ask you to do that, but I like to start with what it would take to get an A in all your planning. Then I can help you backpedal to a good starting point. I think the world of planning is all about progress, not perfection. We want to be better every single year, and we want to move closer to the target. If we don't know what an A+ looks like, then we can't determine a good starting point. So, before I go any further, let me just check in with you. How are you feeling about what we talked about, and what are your thoughts?"

I want to really check in with them, to assess if they're overwhelmed. I want to determine if they're tracking with me, and to know what they're thinking and feeling. I want to know what frightens them, as well as what embarrasses them. I want to provide them a comfort zone to be able to articulate that to me. I want to be empathetic, and I want to listen. If the client truly feels deflated, like, "Man, I have bigger problems than I thought! I thought I was doing better than I am. Now that I've seen your plan, I know I'm way behind, and I don't have near enough money to solve these problems."

This often happens when a client first sees a plan. Typically, at this point, I share a story that goes something like this: "Let's put this in perspective. We just did a plan that looks at your life to make sure that if, God forbid, you don't make it home tonight, your entire family won't miss a beat financially, or if you become fully disabled, your household will survive financially and continue to do well.

"We made sure that you can fully fund four years of undergraduate school for each of your children and that, when you retire at 65, you can retire at 80% of your preretirement income all the way until your 90th birthday. That's what we looked at in the plan.

"Now, Mr. Prospect, let me ask you a question. How many Americans do you think have a plan that does all that and is fully funded? The answer is less than 1%, so I don't want you to feel deflated about not living up to your responsibility as the head of a household. I want you to understand that I'm here to help. The progress we can make together is going to be monumental from what you've done up until this point. It's all about progress, and it's also about a 30- to 35-year journey. When we first got together, I told you I would meet with you every year to review the plan. Every year, we will move the ball down the field further, but we have to start somewhere."

Then, I simply say, "Based on my knowledge and my understanding of your situation, this is exactly where I think we need to start."

After offering my advice, I explain that life and disability insurance requires not only an application, but also some sort of medical exam and perhaps even a monthly check to get the program started. I discuss the uncertainty of how the insurance company will rate the client according to their mortality and morbidity pools.

As such, I explain, "To figure that out, we better get you signed up for a medical exam. We've got to take a blood sample, a urine sample, and answer a bunch of questions. Then you sit back for several weeks while the policy goes through underwriting. They'll contact doctors you have seen in the last couple of years to get your medical file. Once they have that information, and the lab results, they'll make an offer. Once I have that offer, I can come back and sit down with something in stone, and we will know a lot more.

"Today, let's get that process started. When I get back together with you with an offer, we still have the flexibility to make as many changes as we want and go with whatever we decide. Until we have an offer, we can't get started. Is there any reason why we can't schedule that medical exam and fill out the paperwork today?"

At this point, you should have the ball rolling with the paperwork, the applications, and everything moving in the right direction.

If, however, you just can't convince the client to take action, they're simply not ready to move. It is imperative that you do two things. First, set a deadline on the calendar before leaving the meeting to regroup. Second, try your best to determine what they still need to learn and whom they need to talk to so they will feel comfortable making a decision. Ask as many questions and listen as effectively as you can. Then, be able to address those issues and help them in any way possible.

SYSTEM FOR IMPLEMENTATION

1. Begin the meeting by summarizing what was covered in the planning meeting in a clear and concise manner.
2. Start by solving the death benefit need.
3. Have a simple strategy to solve the disability insurance shortage.
4. When addressing their education planning needs, cover the top two to three vehicles available and the pros and cons of each one.
5. When addressing their retirement planning needs, cover the top two to three options available and discuss the pros and cons of each one.
6. Summarize what it would take to fully solve every gap in accordance with their goals.

BRIDGE YOUR GAP • JIM EFFNER

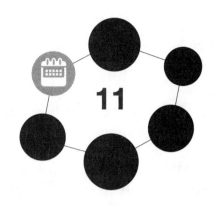

ANNUAL REVIEW

As we begin to look at one of the most important, yet least taught, stages of the sales cycle, we turn to the annual review. When I teach the annual review, I divide it into conceptual components and look down on it from 30,000 feet.

Now, the first component of the annual review focuses on the *client base*. I look at all clients and potential clients in our database.

The second component is what we actually do in the meeting with the client, which is called the annual review.

Let's begin with the client-base component, because I feel it is the most difficult topic to explain and impart to the reps I've worked with.

First, let's define your active book of business. Your active book consists of two groups: the first are all clients who have ever bought anything from you; the second are any clients you completed a fact-finder interview with then entered that information into your system. In other words, they need not have purchased a product from you to be in your system. The reason that might happen is that people buy when they are ready, which may take years.

From my personal practice experience, I can assure you that even the best of clients experience varying financial situations and have different investment timelines. Sometimes you meet a prospect and conduct a solid fact-finding interview, yet it takes two or three years before they buy the first product and become your client. If they measure up to your preferred client standards, you must be patient. You certainly don't want to lose that business if they don't buy immediately, so as we proceed, it's important to be on the same page with the definition of individuals in your book of business. Remember, they don't necessarily have to have bought a product to be included.

Defining Your Book of Business

The controversial area is how many people can be handled in your book of business. I'll start by telling you the number is not black and white. Some argue that it's 400, some say 450, and others might even say 500 if they want to be super active. I've met many successful reps that claim the number is 350. The bottom line is that it's a definitive number, and a point of diminishing returns kicks in once you exceed that number.

Reps often cling to the security blanket that comes

with large numbers. If they add a couple hundred people to their system, they can easily be in the range of 2,000+ clients after a quick 10 years in this business. When I meet reps that have thousands of clients in their system and I tell them they need to get rid of three-quarters of them, the reps think I'm crazy.

The problem is that they have no systematic process of getting in front of those people on a regular basis. The law of large numbers sits in the backdrop for them to cherry pick month-by-month, year-by-year. They sift through the files to figure out who they want to call based on who they think is most likely to buy the next product from them.

This is not only a highly inefficient way to run a financial planning practice, in my humble opinion, it's also not in the best interest of the client. It is borderline unethical. That behavior simply indicates that your business centers on you, not the client. If you have a mentality to see people only when they are ready to buy something, as opposed to serving them to build financial security throughout a lifetime journey, you're clearly not focused on their best interest. You're focused on yours.

Therefore, it's a two-way street – a commitment from both the client and the financial rep. Both parties must meet on an annual basis and relentlessly pursue the promised land of financial security. This becomes a handholding journey filled with challenges, encouragement, and education, sometimes tears, and hopefully joy. In other words, this means going all in and following through on the mission of having long-lasting, intimate relationships with your clients to guide them to financial freedom.

Therefore, the first issue with this new mentality is selectivity. If it's not a numbers game, and we're not looking to build the largest business book possible, we must be very selective. The client number is limited. If your limit is 400 and you sign the 401st client, you need to get rid of one. When we possess that mentality, we become very selective as to whom we let into our database. We target them with a proactive marketing plan and create benchmarks as to what people need to have to get into our practice.

The challenge in this system is that I also preach that a rep should never stop growing. You're either green and growing or ripe and rotting. Therefore, once you get to the number – for now, let's say 400 – for every month you're meeting new people, you want to add those you are excited about to your system, while subtracting those from the bottom who no longer measure up.

Imagine a business book being at a static 400, yet still green and growing. It would contain 400 people for the rest of your career. The quantity would never change, but the quality, measured by net income net worth future potential, would consistently increase.

Often, reps of high integrity struggle with this because they feel they are breaking a promise made to their clients. They feel guilty about getting rid of the ones in the bottom of the funnel over time.

Although this sounds noble, when I've discussed this in depth with more veteran reps, I've learned that they're providing their clients a disservice without knowing it. While they haven't physically deleted the files of those they are not excited about, they have gone years without calling them. This is worse than notifying a client that you've gotten rid of them. When you do not call a client for many years, you must realize that, when other financial advisors call on them, they'll say, "I've already got a guy." They're referring to you, but the reality is they no longer have you. You haven't seen them in years, and you have outdated information on their situation. Thus, you are doing them harm by preventing them from meeting other people who will be more in tune to their needs. This is a disservice, and it must stop.

There are several ways to take care of people you've outgrown. One way is to establish relationships with junior reps who are often thrilled to take on clients who no longer measure up to your specifications. The junior reps will be delighted to continue to serve them.

The second way to handle obsolete clients is to create a client resource center in your network office. There, you can turn over client files to a staff who would service them according to their needs.

The third alternative is to find a replacement rep. Many home offices have 1-800 numbers and service departments that are more than happy to take care of the service needs of neglected clients on an ongoing basis. I suggest simply creating a letter that you feel good about. Upon deciding to quietly file and remove these clients from your system, send them a letter informing them that you made a commitment to them and, if they have any future service needs, you've made appropriate arrangements. Explain that your commitment to service needs will forever be taken care of but, at this point, you see no need to continuously meet. Remember to explain that, if they feel differently, they are welcome to contact you directly.

A Mentality of Abundance

The other important aspect of this stage is your client database perspective. It's critically important to carry the mentality of abundance, as opposed to the theory of scarcity. With the theory of scarcity, it's like the world is going to end. You're desperate, and you feel the need to take anybody who will talk to you. You lack any measurements to determine what makes an acceptable client. You continue to build and stack file upon file as if the world is going to fall apart. The more, the merrier! This perspective brings a false sense of security. It can take your practice to the point where it cannot grow.

The theory of abundance shows you that there are millions of people that you can reach out and talk to, whether it is in a 50-mile radius of your home or around the world. You can work globally via teleconferencing and videoconferencing. Because there are so many people, but only so much time in the day, you must be highly selective as to whom you take. Then, you can go all in with each and every client you accept.

The latter theory is the one you want in the financial planning business. It is the only theory to have if you want to continue to grow.

Why You Should Embrace Annual Reviews

I'd like to share with you a few statistics to illustrate why embracing the annual review, and having a systematic process to get in front of your clients, is so critical. Reps often don't have a systematic way of getting in front of people. Worse, they meet with a new prospective client and work desperately to get them to buy something. Then, if they don't buy anything, they throw the potential client away.

That is a cardinal sin in this business. One-third of your clients will buy *two to three years after the initial meeting*. (Two-thirds of your new clients will buy in the year you meet.) By throwing potential clients away when they don't buy, you're missing a *third* of the people you could potentially sell. That's a statistic worth remembering.

Second, if you successfully sell somebody but they fall through the cracks in your system and you're unable to get back in front of them, you're missing a grand opportunity. Statistics tell us that the average client will buy your core products seven separate times – that includes the risk management products such as life insurance, disability insurance, annuities, and long-term care. Although it might not be politically correct, I like to refer to this process as similar to kissing a girl or boy when you go out on a first date. You don't know each other, so that first kiss is always awkward but, after that, it becomes an afterthought.

It's the same with a new client. It takes approximately 23 hours of effort, eyeball to eyeball, to sell a new client – but the second sale takes less than three hours. Every sale after that requires slightly less time as you build a relationship. Build trust, and people will do what you tell them to do easier and quicker once they become a client.

So, we want to use that knowledge to our advantage and make sure we capture all seven of those sales. Your best clients will buy 12 or 13 times from you, so failing to have any systematic process to get in front of these people is a tremendous mistake.

The second statistic I want to share with you is so fascinating that most people don't believe me at first. It relates to risk management products and the underlying premium sold in those products; every single sale is greater in premium than the summation of all the previous sales.

Let me offer an example. If you're selling somebody for the fourth time, on average the premium of that fourth sale will outweigh the premium of the first, second, and third sale combined. Now, I know when you read that, you're baffled and probably don't believe it. Allow me to explain.

As it relates to selling risk management products, the lower-end premium products can be bought simply through logic alone. For example, if you meet a young family with no life insurance and you help them understand the necessary amount of life insurance – let's say that's $1 million on the breadwinner and $250,000 on the stay-at-home spouse – it's a logical decision to buy that in term insurance. At a very low premium, they'll pull the trigger on that rather quickly.

However, to persuade them to buy a big chunk of permanent insurance and spend thousands of dollars on annual premiums, that is accomplished through building trust. Trust is earned over time, so life insurance clients are much more prone to buy term insurance early on, before converting to permanent insurance as they begin to trust the advisor. That's why the premiums get bigger and bigger as time goes by.

Now you can imagine by these stats alone that, if you lack a process to get in front of your clients on a systematic basis, you are missing a tremendous opportunity. I often equate this mistake to reps banging their head against the wall over and over. Without a system to get in front of your clients, each successive year is like your first year in the business.

One of the multiple beauties of this business is that it's designed to get easier year after year. If you fail to embrace this concept, you are not taking advantage of that fundamental principle, and it is time you change.

So, now that we agree you can serve a limited number of clients, let's move on to your role during the annual review.

I love Stephen Covey's principle of "beginning with the end in mind," so, before discussing the annual review goals, I'd like to be crystal clear on what we want to accomplish. In other words, I want to specify our objectives in the review.

The first objective is making the client feel as though we've taken complete ownership of their journey to long-term financial security. We will talk about that briefly in this perspective.

As a child, if you grew up in a loving and caring household, hopefully your parents took a considerable interest in helping you understand the importance of money. Perhaps they taught you how to open a checking account, a savings account, and how to manage your money wisely. Perhaps even into your 20s, they cared about whether you handled your finances the right way. But once you started raising a family and ventured out in the real world, most parents step away, and financial security planning can become an extremely lonely job.

Typically, nobody else cares about your financial security except, perhaps, your spouse. Within this lonely setting, a financial rep can position themselves as an advocate for a family's long-term financial security. The rep can create a vision that will inspire a family sit down at the table every year to do an annual review.

Your Role During the Annual Review

You'll want to put your arms around them, hold their hand, kick them in the butt, slap them high fives, give them knowledge, teach them, and be there for them. The relationship becomes a partnership, which is very welcomed by most clients. You want your clients to feel as if you're right there with them on this journey. Conducting an annual review accomplishes that objective.

We want to appear very well organized, extremely professional, and very thorough to our clients. Keeping accurate case notes and reviewing them every single year with the clients remind them what you talked about a year ago, two years ago, even three years ago, and show their accomplishments and outstanding goals. This embodies the principles of organization, professionalism, and thoroughness, and that is also what we want to accomplish.

We want our clients to feel continuity in our planning process from where they started, to where they are going. They want to know that we have a plan and that there's light at the end of the tunnel. As I've noted in multiple sections of this book, financial security is a 30- or 40-year journey.

As we begin this process, we cannot do everything for clients, but we need to have a philosophy as to where we start and how we proceed throughout that journey. Our clients need to feel like they're on the right track and heading in the right direction. The annual review helps accomplish this.

We want to capture all the additional sales, too. As I mentioned earlier, the average client buys seven separate times. Through an annual review, we open additional cases and close them, most importantly, for the benefit of the client to move the ball down the field toward the end zone of security. It also positively impacts our business as we strive to capture all those sales, which represent another objective of our annual review.

Last but not least, it is almost as important as everything else to get referrals and be well nominated to the client's inner circle. As we perform great work with our clients and they see success in the annual review, they are much more likely to introduce us to their most trusted friends and family members – their inner circle. That's where they have the most influence. Those are the people they love and care about the most, and those are the referrals we want.

Setting Up the Annual Review

So, let's start with the first principle: every client, every year. This reaffirms why you must limit the number of people in your practice.

I use two techniques to make sure I get in front of my clients. The first has nothing to do with the annual review; yet, it is still very important: the birthday call. I like to call my clients on their birthdays. In my early years in the business, I read an article in a financial planning journal about a poll conducted among a group of clients. The poll asked clients to name the top five things they disliked about their financial advisors, and the clients' top complaint was that advisors only called them when they wanted to sell something.

You know the old saying, "The truth hurts"? That really hit home with me, because not only did it sound bad when I read it, but upon examining my practice it rang true. I was guilty. I was cherry picking and didn't want to waste my time. My practice centered entirely on me. I had no long-term vision and focused solely on the next sale.

I knew I needed to make a change, so I instituted the birthday call. The birthday call turned out to be one of my greatest decisions, simply because it not only defied the "truth hurts" principle, it also became something I found incredibly enjoyable.

At the beginning of each month, I identify all my clients with birthdays that month, and I call them on their birthdays (or on Friday if their birthday falls on the weekend).

My birthday greetings are virtually identical, but before sharing that with you, I'll point out that prior to each call, I pull the client's file. In my case notes from our last annual review, I find answers to personal questions I asked clients to know them better and learn their story. I capture the highlights of those notes and review them before making that birthday call. My call might be brief, but my one rule is *no business discussion whatsoever.* The call is simply to build our relationship and reinforce the idea that I want to connect without selling them financial products.

So, I'll call the client and say, "Mr. Prospect, it's Jim. My goal this morning is to be the first to wish you happy birthday. Did I accomplish my goal?"

Usually they'll say that their spouse wished them a happy birthday before they left for work, so I'll laugh about that and say, "Well, I hope I'm at least number two. How are you doing?"

Then I'll reference something from their file. Let's say their daughter last year was trying out for the middle school cheerleading team. Armed with this information, I may say, "Hey, did Becky make the cheerleading team last year? How's she doing?" That personal touch will deepen our relationship even if the call lasts only six or seven minutes. At the end of the call, I'll convey how much I appreciate having them in my practice and say that I'm looking forward to the annual review six months down the road. Finally, I wish them the best on this special day.

If I'm unable to reach a client – which happens probably three-quarters of the time – I leave a happy birthday voicemail, thank them for being my client, and tell them I look forward to seeing them at the annual review. That marks a great decision in my career, and I'm certain it had a lot to do with building excellent relationships with my clients.

We now move on to the annual review. I found it best to schedule the review six months after a client's birthday, thereby touching base with them twice a year, spread apart by six months. That system works well for me – feel free to borrow it if it fits you, too.

Six months after the birthday call, the reminder would simply come up in my system, which leads me to the second thing I want to teach you. When you call the client for the annual review, there is no cherry picking – no perception of, "Well, they bought a bunch last year. They're probably not buying for a while, so I'm going to pass them over." Remember the first principle for the annual review: every client, every year, face-to-face.

If the client is not worth your time when you look at the file, you must quiet that file. In other words, get rid of them in whatever system you have created to get rid of your clients. This should happen on a monthly basis once you get to that magic number – for now, let's say that number is, again, 400 people. For every month you add accounts, you need to delete accounts from your system. The clients you should remove are those you're not excited about when they come up for the annual review. Make sure you have a process for that.

The second aspect of the annual review is your language.

Everyone has his or her own idea as to who should do this. In my practice, I called all new clients from referrals and any others I wanted to meet for the first time. My staff called all existing clients in my system for the annual review.

The language should be very simple. Your staff does not want to deal with conflict, and they aren't salespeople, so it should simply sound like this:

"Hello, Mr. Prospect, this is such-and-such, Jim Effner's assistant. I just wanted to let you know that it's time for your annual review, and I was wondering if next Tuesday or Wednesday would be better for you at 2 o'clock in our office."

The client can schedule – or they may make up an excuse. The first time, they often make excuses.

"Well, nothing has changed. I don't need to get together with Jim now."

"I'm really busy."

"I'm not interested now. I'll see him next year."

"I don't really see any benefit right now."

Before teaching you how to deal with that, I want to teach you to be very introspective about what clients are actually telling you. What they're saying is they don't see much value in what you bring to the table. If a client only wants to see you when they need to purchase a product from you, this indicates that they do not view you as an advisor but as simply a sales person who distributes product.

In these cases, my assistant simply says, "Okay, why don't I have Jim follow up with you?"

Those files are brought to my office, and I personally call those clients. I say something like this:

"Mr. Prospect, it's Jim. My assistant called you and mentioned that you weren't interested in getting together for an annual review. I just wanted to follow up and see what was going on in your mind."

About half the time, they would say, "You know what? I thought about it. Let's get together." The change came simply from hearing my voice.

However, they might proceed by repeating what they told my assistant. I simply reply with, "You know what, Mr. Prospect? I apologize. Maybe I didn't make myself clear when we first met, and I told you that it's a very important process in my practice for me to get together with clients each year for an annual review. The reason for that is because I take my responsibility seriously, and I need to build a relationship with my clients. Things change in life, both in family and finances, in careers and objectives and goals. If I'm not together with my clients on an annual basis, I don't feel I can do my job. I'm not interested in only whether things have changed or whether you need to do anything. What I'm interested in is building a relationship with you and helping you achieve long-term financial security. Having said that, what time next week works well for you for your annual review?"

If they push back after that, I have a very direct conversation and inform the client I'm no longer interested in working with them.

See, when you say you stand for something, you have to be willing to fall on your sword for it when tested. If not, you don't truly stand for your principles. This is where the rubber hits the road on your value system. From my perspective, if someone is my client, I will do the best job I possibly can, and they're damn lucky to have me as a financial rep. If they're not serious enough about their planning to sit down with me just once a year, I'm no longer interested in being their financial representative.

When I share this with reps, it blows them away, but I promise you will experience a transformational amount of growth through this perspective. The first time you fire somebody, you will feel like a million bucks. Carry that self-confidence with you. It'll pay back in spades.

I did that once with the client, and every year after, they scheduled the annual review with my assistant. It is only with a new client on the first annual review call that we have to push for a meeting. Even then, we only have to do it occasionally.

Annual Review Preparation

The third step in the annual review is developing a system for meeting preparation. One week in advance, I thoroughly review the client's file. A thorough review would include things like:

- Reading all the case notes

- Reviewing all the updated statements of any products bought from me over time

- Reviewing the results of all referrals they've given me

I also developed a meeting prep checklist. My staff owns this process, and they put a check in each of the boxes to make sure that I have included the following items.

Annual Review Prep Checklist

☐ I have a financial planning checklist

☐ I have a copy of the plan that we have been developing over the years

☐ I have an updated statement of all the products they own with me, both investment assets and risk management products

☐ I have a list of the referrals that they've given me and notes of what happened with each of these

My staff completes the check, and I review the file before the meeting. I always feel very confident that everything was done correctly, and I show up fully prepared. This helps me look professional and gets my clients feeling that much better about working with me.

The fourth step in the annual review brings consistency to your meetings – use an identical meeting agenda for all annual reviews.

The agenda I suggest begins by providing the client an executive summary of the prior meeting. As it's been a year since the previous meeting, reading all your case notes brings them back up to speed. Talk about your discussion in the review a year ago, what action they took, and it'll bring them back as if you met a week ago.

Second, I present an overview of the financial planning checklist. Go over all the statements of all the products they have with you. The checklist is important for the following reasons:

1. It shows the progress they've made.
2. It shows how much more work you still have to do.

I think this is important for a couple of reasons. Once again, you want the client to see and feel that there's a light at the end of the tunnel. As you progress in your relationship, the light starts to burn brighter and brighter. I often like to highlight with my clients their progress, because I have found they sometimes feel frustrated and almost like they haven't accomplished much. When you can remind them of what they had when you first met and what they have after a brief four or five years into the relationship, they realize that they've made significant progress – and they wouldn't have made much of it without you.

The second is helping the client understand how much more work they need to do. This just reinforces the need for the annual reviews, as well as a level of relentless pursuit to guide them to total financial security.

Next on the agenda is to update the client's fact-finder and get all the new data. It's been a year since you met them. Their income has likely changed, hopefully increased. Their assets have changed; maybe they changed jobs, family status, or whatever. We want to update all their information. This is no different than doing a new fact-finder with a new client.

As taught in the fact-finder module, the fact-finder process is completed with a discovery agreement that carries the three C's: It's clear, concise, and compelling. It should articulate what you just covered and the areas you need to address next, so the client feels compelled to get back together soon to continue moving forward with you as their financial advisor. Summarize in the meeting that you're outlining the next steps and setting the next appointment for the next purchase, to continue their journey toward financial security.

The next agenda item is updating the client's goals. They have stated their goals in the past, but sometimes those change. We want to make sure they remain consistent.

The last step in the annual review is prospecting and getting referrals. I like to start by going through any referrals they've provided in the past. I want to tell them about what's happened with each one, and I genuinely thank them for any that have become clients or are close to becoming clients.

If they've never given me referrals, but I've asked, I'll ask a little differently. For example, I might say, "You know, Mr. Prospect, meeting new people is the lifeline of my business. I know I've asked you in the past and, for one reason or another, we haven't been successful in identifying people. I'd like to think by now I've earned your trust and the ability to be introduced to people that you genuinely care about."

Then I proceed to prospect with them.

This is a relentless pursuit I've cultivated to the point that my clients become programmed. They know at the end of that meeting I'm going to do it. Typically, my clients begin coming to meetings prepared with a couple of referrals written on a piece of paper. They simply hand them to me before I even ask at the end of a meeting. That's when you know you're making progress with your clients.

Mastering the Annual Review

So, we've covered a lot in this annual review. Specifically, we've talked about what it takes for an individual to be in your system and what you need to do in the annual review. I've found that annual reviews are one of the most enjoyable parts of my practice. They are truly the conduits toward transforming a prospective client who may be defensive in fear of a sales pitch or who views your profession negatively.

The annual review can develop that reluctance into an intimate relationship that brings a great deal of pride and enjoyment, along with a trusted, valuable advisor, into the client's life. The conduit between those two extremes is the annual review, and it becomes that much more apparent after you've completed multiple reviews. This business is very rewarding when you reach the point that clients genuinely appreciate and respect the work you do for them. It's in the annual review where you start to see this and progressively see it more as you conduct more annual reviews.

I ask that you choose wisely, not only based on the quality of the clients you work with, but on the *quality of relationships* that you develop with them. When you look at a file prior to an annual review, if you're genuinely excited about getting together with that person because you enjoy being with them – and you have that feeling with 100% of your clients – that's when you know you're close to tapping into the full potential the good Lord gave you, as well as the true rewards and benefits of this business.

Also, it must be pointed out that if you are in the early stage of your career, it is imperative that you focus on activity and building clients. You have to earn the right to be selective over time.

Good luck in this pursuit. Before I go, I have one last thought to share from my quarter century of experience.

Other than prospecting, the single biggest issue I've seen reps struggle with is filling their calendar. Most reps feel that, if they could get in front of enough people every month, they could meet all their goals, but they struggle to fill their calendars. It's a constant battle, and they never come close to their capacity.

Let me leave you with another concept. Do the math, keeping the numbers simple, and assume you've decided you can support 360 people. If you embrace my concept of every client, every year, and we assume that every client birthday is spread out equally – which, by the way, would never happen – then you will call 30 people every month for annual reviews. That's 30 kept appointments solely from your annual reviews. You'll probably open additional cases and return to the implementation planning stages in that same month with at least half your clients, which equates to another 15 appointments. Now you're up to 45 appointments.

If you're doing the necessary work, you will take a minimum of 12 new fact-finder appointments every month. Now you're up to 57 kept appointments before factoring in anything else.

It's like the flywheel concept in Jim Collins' book *Good to Great*. It took forever to get the flywheel going. As a new rep, you were so desperate you resorted to cold calling. Now you've embraced this system to build your clientele and honor the review. It's almost as though you need to get out of your own way because the wheel spins faster and faster without any effort. You're keeping 55 to 60+ appointments a month, and you're really reaping the fruits of your labor.

Good luck with this concept!

SYSTEM FOR ANNUAL REVIEW

1. Have a system for meeting with every single client at least once a year.
2. Use consistent language to set up the annual review and overcome potential objections.
3. Use a process that allows you to be completely prepared for the meeting.
4. Follow a meeting agenda that begins with an executive summary of past meetings, updates their information, and uses a financial planning checklist to review the current status of their financial planning goals.
5. Utilize consistent language that effectively summarizes the annual review, defines the next steps, and schedules the next appointment.
6. Provide an updated status on all referrals provided by your client, thank them for the successful ones, and prospect for more.

BRIDGE YOUR GAP • JIM EFFNER

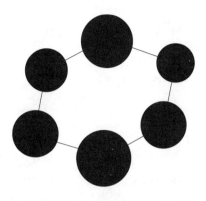

FINAL NOTE: NOW YOU'RE READY...

So, there you have it! You have now been exposed to most of what I have accomplished and learned in my 27 years as a professional financial salesperson. We have covered just about everything relating to financial sales. Starting from how to process a name and get it on a referral lead basis, to how to make the appointment, to how to build it on your calendar, to how to conduct a successful fact-finder meeting. I put together a plan to help you close the Gap and conduct an annual review.

You now have a system for each one of those steps, along with all the tools necessary to start to tap into your true potential. I hope my personal stories and struggles served to inspire your journey. We all need a little inspiration and the feeling of camaraderie in this business, so I hope you will pick up this book when you feel your Gap starting to expand and your tank getting a little low.

I want to now talk about executing the methods I outline, but, before we start on execution, we have to first begin with your mindset.

Your mindset is really categorized in a couple of different areas. The first area is *belief*. The real question is: Do you believe in yourself? And equally important, do you believe in what you do and what you deliver? Many people get confused as to what it is that they really do, especially when they don't focus on what their clients really want.

Let me give you an interesting example of this. There are more than 1 million people each year who enter hardware stores to buy quarter inch drill bits. Yet, not one of those people actually *want* a quarter inch drill bit. What they want is a quarter inch *hole*, but they must buy the drill bit in order to drill the hole.

Are you in tune with what your clients truly want? Are you talking about what they actually desire from a financial planner? Do you focus on the drill bit, or do you focus on the hole your client actually wants?

The real take-away here, though, is not what you talk about, but how deeply do you believe in what you deliver? I have learned a lot over my career, and one of the lessons at the top of the list is this: Our beliefs drive our behaviors. So, before we start to change our behaviors and execute the systems we have learned throughout this entire book, we must start on what you believe.

Here's what I want you to believe: Your clients and your

potential clients *need you*, desperately. People don't save. People don't plan. People don't have a trusted advisor. Therefore, people travel on a road of financial destruction unless they have someone like you in their lives. You need to believe that what you do is a noble cause, and that the difference you make is incredibly important. The more people you work with and the high quality in which you conduct your craft will have a dramatic, exponential impact on the communities in which you live in and for the clients you serve. That's what I want you to believe. And remind yourself of this every day.

Next, I want you to believe in *yourself*. Expressed throughout the entire book is the concept of how, unlike the professional sports field, the medical field, or the legal world, you do not need any special genetic wiring to succeed. If you can read this book, you have what it takes to be highly successful in the financial services industry. You simply have to learn how to get comfortable with the uncomfortable. You have to fill yourself with courage, and it has to be connected to what you truly believe in. Belief in yourself is an essential component of your success. Even though it starts with beliefs, it will ultimately transfer into the confidence that your clients will perceive.

Throughout my years, I've learned confidence can be broken down into two categories: knowledge and skill set. There is an inherent instinct in every human to want to not look stupid. Therefore, if you lack knowledge, fear will hold you back from discussing important subjects openly and honestly, because you will be worried clients will want to discuss subjects or ask questions that you cannot answer.

The good news is that this industry is not rocket science. You do not have to go to school for four years to learn what you need in order to deliver value from an intellectual horsepower standpoint. However, you do need to take the time to learn the essentials, because with that knowledge comes empowerment and confidence. And more, happier clients!

The second part of confidence is your skill set. The great news is that I've just delivered this to you from start to finish in this book. You now have the manual. You know exactly what it is that you need to do to move someone to action. From the very beginning of the sales cycle, all the way to the end, you can become a master at your craft.

Practice it with relentless pursuit, and when you take a combination of your knowledge, the craft, and skills that you bring to the table, you will exponentially grow the muscle of confidence necessary for your full potential.

The next dimension of this process has to be your awareness. There will be a direct correlation from your habits to your results. This business is not one where we have to get lucky. This business is not one that requires you that you are at the right place at the right time. It is not one where the moon and the stars need to line up perfectly. Thank goodness for that! Every single individual who taps into their full potential and understands what is needed to put forth in effort and activity will succeed in this business. That activity, when coupled with the right mindset and a strong skill set, always leads to a predictable positive result.

Therefore, I encourage you to tap into your own mindset

as it relates to your activity and then ask yourself: Is my current activity in alignment with my full potential? Make sure you're clear on that before you move forward. If your answer is no, change your habits immediately to align with the concepts I outlined.

Something else that is important about mindset is that it's really all about expectations. I want you to break that down to two components. The first one is what you expect of yourself. The second is what you expect of your clients. The genesis of my company, the P2P Group, started on my insatiable appetite of curiosity about the enormous Gap between the average financial services professional's success and what they are capable of producing on an annual basis.

I believe, and am continuously proven right, that the average financial services individual taps into only 10% of their potential. When you do the math and you meet with the amount of people you should, and when you master the craft of favorable introductions and being well nominated, you will slowly but surely increase the caliber of the individuals you meet, and your future will become unlimited.

In more than 3,500 fact-finding interviews that I completed in the first 12 years of my career, I can literally count on one hand the rare individuals that had every "i" dotted and every "t" crossed. Almost every individual that I have met had a Gap in his or her plan somewhere. Everyone you meet with needs your help. Every time you meet with someone, it is an opportunity to enable them to become financially secure. There is a huge amount of possibility with every fact-finder meeting. Therefore, what you once expected of yourself in terms of productivity needs to be blown up. The new expectation has to be progressively larger year after year after year.

I want you to liken it to the stretching of a rubber band to the point that it never goes back to its original form. When you start to stretch it to see what's possible, you can transform yourself from the first stage, which is the impossible, to the second stage, which is the possible, to the third stage, which is the probable. Then you repeat that process over and over again.

After all, what's the alternative? Just getting by? Just going through the motions? That attitude of doing "just enough" will certainly lead to all sorts of regrets, take it from me. When it's all said and done, I encourage you to really tap into your potential and take this thing to the moon! At the risk of sounding cliché, I want you to believe the world is your oyster. After reading this book and applying the tools, the expectations you have for yourself should be far greater than you could have ever even *comprehended* before.

I encourage you to go out there with a fresh start. I encourage you to embrace a new horizon of goals and vision. Finally, I encourage you to go make a difference, for yourself and for everybody that you meet. Embrace this strategy because you are special, important, and what you do will change lives, starting with your own!

Good luck and God bless.